OXFORD *Playscripts*

Bram Stoker

adapted by David Calcutt

Dracula

Oxford University Press

OXFORD

UNIVERSITY PRESS

Great Clarendon Street, Oxford OX2 6DP

Oxford University Press is a department of the University of Oxford.
It furthers the University's objective of excellence in research, scholarship,
and education by publishing worldwide in

Oxford New York

Auckland Bangkok Buenos Aires Cape Town Chennai
Dar es Salaam Delhi Hong Kong Istanbul Karachi Kolkata
Kuala Lumpur Madrid Melbourne Mexico City Mumbai Nairobi
São Paulo Shanghai Taipei Tokyo Toronto

Oxford is a registered trade mark of Oxford University Press
in the UK and in certain other countries

This adaptation of *Dracula* © David Calcutt 1999

Activity section © Fiona Edwards 1999

The moral rights of the authors have been asserted

Database right Oxford University Press (maker)

First published 1999
Reprinted 2000, 2001, 2002 (twice)

Printed at The Alden Press Ltd., Oxford

ISBN 0 19 831456 6

The Publisher would like to thank the following for permission to reproduce photographs:
pp 107, 110 Mary Evans Picture Library, p 111 Gamma/Christophe Rove,
p 124 Ronald Grant Archive (top), Kobal Collection/Granata Press Service (bottom),
p 125 Kobal Collection, p 126 Ronald Grant Archive.

Front cover by Simon Fell
Inside illustrations by Peter Melnyczuk

Contents

Characters

In order of their
appearance on stage:

Count Dracula	*a Transylvanian aristocrat, also a vampire*
Jonathan Harker	*a young lawyer, engaged to Mina*
Mr Hawkins	*a solicitor, Jonathan's employer*
Landlady	*at the Golden Krone Hotel in Bistritz, Transylvania*
Lost girl	*whom Jonathan meets on his way to Castle Dracula*
Mina Murray	*an intelligent young woman, engaged to Jonathan*
Lucy Westenra	*Mina's friend since childhood, lives in Whitby*
Dr John Seward	*a young doctor in charge of a large asylum in Whitby, one of Lucy's admirers*
Quincey Morris	*a well-travelled young American, a friend of John Seward and Arthur Holmwood, also admires Lucy*
Arthur Holmwood	*only son of Lord Godalming, engaged to Lucy*
Hag 1 **Hag 2** **Hag 3**	*hideous creatures at Castle Dracula*
Mr Swales	*Whitby's oldest inhabitant*
Reporter	*on Whitby's newspaper*
Coastguard	*at Whitby*
Renfield	*a patient at Doctor Seward's asylum*

Bennett
Withers } *attendants who work at the asylum*

Mrs Westenra   *Lucy's mother*

Professor Van Helsing   *once Doctor Seward's tutor, an expert on vampires*

Child   *who plays in the abbey churchyard as it gets dark*

Mrs Outhwaite   *caretaker at Carfax Manor*

Before You Read the Play

Before you read the play, you might find it useful to know what I had in mind when I wrote the script. The story of **Dracula** unfolds in two ways:

- through a number of narrators who describe the events as they experienced them
- by showing the actual events as they happen.

I have kept the set design, the props, the lighting instructions, and the stage directions to a minimum in the script – and the play can be read aloud in the classroom or performed for an audience successfully using these directions alone. But there are occasions, particularly during the narrated sections of the playscript, when you may decide that additional movement, mime or props are appropriate. This is a decision for each individual teacher or director to make.

Equally, you may choose to use more scenery, furniture and props, special effects (such as dry ice) or sound than I have suggested; or you may have a sophisticated lighting system at your disposal (the existing lighting directions are there simply as a guide). Again, the decision as to how you produce your performance of **Dracula** is up to you, and the structure of this playscript allows for this.

Description of the set

There should be a large French window with double doors at the centre rear of the stage. This can be hidden by a large deep red curtain, and revealed when it is needed – as in the scenes where Dracula enters and exits through the window to appear to both Lucy and Mina. Other characters (including Dracula, where appropriate) enter and exit from the sides of the stage, which should be hung with large red drapes. A bench or seat should be placed just off to one side of the window, to the stage left.

David Calcutt

Act 1

Prologue

*The lights rise. **Dracula** enters and speaks to the audience.*

Dracula   For centuries I have walked my world alone. In fierce joy, but in weariness too. The weariness of solitude. For so long I have yearned for a companion to share with me this world, this eternity. And I shall walk alone no more. One shall walk beside me. One shall become my companion. Here, beneath this sky lit by its numberless stars, we shall stand together, and gaze towards the black shadows of the mountains. And we shall be filled with hunger and silent longing, and the moon shall rise, and we shall be wolves running, with the horizons rolling endlessly beneath our feet.

* *

Dracula goes.

Scene 1

Jonathan Harker enters carrying a briefcase. He puts this down and speaks to the audience.

Jonathan   It began when I was working as an assistant lawyer in the offices of Mr Hawkins, the solicitor. And it was in connection with that work, and from Mr Hawkins's own lips, that I first heard the name of Dracula.

Mr Hawkins enters, carrying a file of papers. He speaks to Jonathan.

Mr Hawkins   He lives in Eastern Europe. A small country called Transylvania. Ever heard of it?

Jonathan turns to Mr Hawkins.

Jonathan   No, I can't say that I have.

Mr Hawkins	Neither had I. It doesn't matter. Bohemia, Moravia, Muldavia, Transylvania – all places on a map between here and there, if you know what I mean.
Jonathan	Yes...
Mr Hawkins	Anyway, this Dracula fellow lives there. An aristocrat. Old family, going all the way back to the time of Attila the Hun, or something like that. And the point is, he wants to move to England. Fallen in love with the place, by all accounts. All from books, mind. Never been here. No doubt he'll find the reality a bit different.
Jonathan	No doubt.
Mr Hawkins	None of his craggy mountains and pine forests and wild landscapes here. Corner shops and trolley-buses. And rain. We mustn't forget the rain. Not that we could if we tried. (*Pause*) Where was I?
Jonathan	You were telling me about Mr Dracula.
Mr Hawkins	Count, Count Dracula, my boy. No plain 'Mr' for him. Oh, dear me, no. These European chaps can be very touchy about their ancestry and titles. Remember that when you meet him.
Jonathan	I'm to meet him?
Mr Hawkins	Yes. That's what I'm coming to. You see, he got in touch with me a while back through an agent of his – can't remember the man's name. English, he was. Very excitable, though. Couldn't keep still. Made my head spin just to speak with him. Well, this agent brought me a letter from the Count stating that he wished to move to England and he wanted a reliable firm to find a place for him. Money no object. A reliable firm, my boy. And he chose us. How's that, eh?
Jonathan	Your reputation's travelled far indeed, Mr Hawkins.
Mr Hawkins	So it would appear. And so shall you, Jonathan. You shall travel with it. All the way to Transylvania!
Jonathan	What? I'm to go there?

Mr Hawkins	Yes! That's what I'm trying to tell you. I think I've found just the kind of place Count Dracula is looking for. Not an easy task, I can tell you. He was very particular in his requirements. *Very* particular. Quite odd, some of them, too. Still, it's not my place to comment on a client's wishes. Especially when that client is paying so handsomely.
Jonathan	Where is the place you've found?
Mr Hawkins	Oh. It's in the north. Whitby.
Jonathan	(*Surprised*) Really?
Mr Hawkins	Do you know it?
Jonathan	No, but my fiancée is going there this summer, to stay with an old friend of hers.
Mr Hawkins	Coincidence, eh? She'll come across this place. Carfax Manor, it's called. A bit of a ruin, really, but that's what he asked for. Something old and spacious and remote. Well, Carfax Manor is certainly old and spacious, and you can't get much more remote than Whitby!
Jonathan	You've written and told the Count?
Mr Hawkins	I have, and he's written back, and asked me to travel to his home with all the details and documents. As if it were like hopping into a cab across town. I'm too old for such a journey, but you're not, so I'm sending you in my place. It's about time you saw something of the world.
Jonathan	I'm very grateful, Mr Hawkins. To be entrusted with such a responsibility – it's... a great honour.
Mr Hawkins	I wouldn't send you if I didn't think you were up to it, Jonathan. And you are. You're more than up to it. Why, sending you is like going myself. You have my every confidence. I've written a letter to the Count and told him so.
Jonathan	Thank you.

Mr Hawkins hands the file to Jonathan.

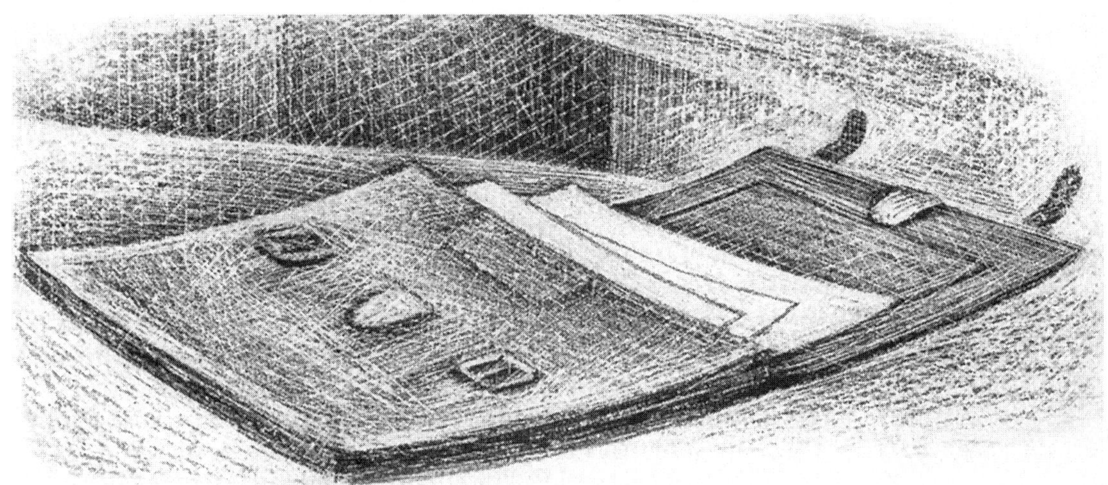

Hawkins	Everything's in there – details and specifications of the property, a photograph of it that I took myself, copies of the deeds, documents – and contracts. Most importantly the contracts. There are three for him to sign. And there are travel arrangements sent by the Count. Study everything carefully. Put aside your other duties and devote yourself to this task. Have it all by heart by the time you arrive there. He'll expect as much, and so shall I.
Jonathan	When shall I leave?
Mr Hawkins	As soon as possible. Next week, if you can. The sooner you go, the sooner you'll be there, and the sooner back with everything signed and sealed. And then... well, I think you might have cause for celebration. And I'm not just talking about your forthcoming marriage. I'm looking for a partner, you know. Someone to run the business with me. Do well in this, and there'll be cause for celebration indeed.
Jonathan	(*Deeply grateful*) Thank you, Mr Hawkins.
Mr Hawkins	We'll talk further when you return. It's all in your hands, now.

> **Mr Hawkins** *turns to go. He stops and turns back.*

Mr Hawkins	It's a great opportunity for you, my boy. A great opportunity. Yes. And a great adventure!

Mr Hawkins *goes.* **Jonathan** *puts the file in his briefcase and as he does so he speaks to the audience.*

Jonathan   A great adventure. So it seemed to me, too. Even the distress I felt at having to part from Mina, my fiancée, couldn't quell my sense of excitement and anticipation. And we told each other that it wouldn't be for long, and that, when I returned, we'd be married. So I left the next week, took the boat from Calais, went on to Paris, travelled by train to Munich, then onward to Budapest. From there, my journey was by coach, along roads increasingly remote, which wound their way through the Carpathian mountains. And at last, among the lower slopes of those mountains, I arrived at my penultimate destination, the town of Bistritz, and the Golden Krone Hotel, where I was to stay before setting out on the final stage of my journey.

The **landlady** *enters and approaches Jonathan. She speaks with an Eastern European accent.*

Landlady   English?

Jonathan   Yes, that's right.

Landlady   It's a long way you've come. England is far from here.

Jonathan   It is. Very far.

Landlady   You speak good German.

Jonathan   Thank you.

Landlady   A good job. There's no one speaks English here. How long will you stay?

Jonathan   Just the one night. I have to go on, tomorrow, through the Borgo Pass. Is there a coach that will take me?

Landlady   Yes, there is a coach. It leaves here at four tomorrow afternoon, to Bukovina. Is that where you're going?

Jonathan   No. I only wish to go as far as the Borgo Pass.

Landlady	But there is nothing there.
Jonathan	I was told there's a road that leads to the Castle Dracula.

*The **landlady** starts a little.*

Landlady	Castle Dracula?
Jonathan	Yes. That's where I'm going. You know it?
Landlady	I know it.
Jonathan	And there is a road – ?
Landlady	A track. It is not easy to walk.
Jonathan	Is it far, though? To the castle?
Landlady	(*Hesitantly*) No…
Jonathan	Then I'm sure I'll manage –
Landlady	But the pass is many hours away. It will be dark when you get there.
Jonathan	I don't mind.
Landlady	If I'm permitted to ask, why do you go to Castle Dracula?
Jonathan	I have business with the Count.
Landlady	Business. Must you go there tomorrow?
Jonathan	Yes, I must.
Landlady	Stay here. One night is such a short time. Our town is beautiful. Stay a little longer, two nights. Go the day after tomorrow.
Jonathan	I wish I could. Your town does indeed look very beautiful. But my business is quite pressing. Perhaps when I come back –
Landlady	Do you know what tomorrow is?

Jonathan	It's the... fourth of May –
Landlady	St George's Eve. On that day, and on that night, the evil things of the world have sway. They rise, they walk abroad, they are strong in their power. And that place to which you are going –

She stops.

Jonathan	What of it?
Landlady	It is old. Many dead lie in its roots. It has eaten much blood.
Jonathan	Look, I... I'm afraid I don't believe in such things...
Landlady	No, not in your land, perhaps. You have no need. But here there is need. It is not your land. It is ours, and here such things are real.

Jonathan *turns and speaks to the audience.*

Jonathan	Despite her obvious concern, I insisted I must travel on the next day. And seeing my determination, she fell silent, and showed me to my room. I passed a quiet night, and a pleasant morning, and she spoke no more of her fears, until the carriage arrived, and I prepared to take my leave.

*The **landlady** speaks to Jonathan.*

Landlady	You are certain about going? You are decided?
Jonathan	Yes, I am.
Landlady	Then take this.

She takes a small crucifix on a chain from her pocket and offers it to Jonathan.

Landlady	It is a cross, the sign of Our Lord and Saviour.
Jonathan	Really, I couldn't –
Landlady	Please. Take it. For your safety. It will protect you.

*She makes to fasten the cross around
Jonathan's neck. He speaks sharply.*

Jonathan   No! I mean... (*Changing his tone*) Yes, I will take it, thank
you... you're very kind...

He takes the crucifix from her.

Landlady   Keep it with you at all times.

Jonathan   I will.

Landlady   And may God and His Holy Mother be with you, and keep
you from evil.

*The **landlady** turns and goes. **Jonathan**
looks at the crucifix and speaks to the
audience.*

Jonathan   I placed the crucifix in my pocket, and forgot about it. And I
must have lost it, for I never saw it again.

*He puts the crucifix in his pocket and picks
up his briefcase. He then continues his story.*

Jonathan   Within a short time of leaving the town, the sun began to set.
As we climbed higher through the pass, the mountains were
bathed in a deep red light, and the sky darkened above them,
filling the whole world about me in shadow. Then I slept, and
woke to darkness and black night. The carriage had stopped.
We had reached the top of the Borgo Pass. I got out, found the
road easily enough, and began my ascent to Castle Dracula.
The landlady of the hotel had been right. It was hard going,
especially at night. And cold, too. Bitterly cold. It was a
cloudless night and the moon was full. In the distance I heard
wolves howling. Once, I thought I saw a light flickering among
the rocks above me. A pale-blue, unearthly light. I left the path
and climbed towards it, but it disappeared, and as I turned to
make my way back to the road, there was a movement in the
shadows, and a figure stood before me.

*The **lost girl** enters and approaches
Jonathan. She is dressed in rags and her face
is hidden by a hood.*

Lost girl	Help me.

> *Jonathan* turns to her, but continues to speak to the audience.

Jonathan	It was a girl – or young woman –
Lost girl	Will you help me?
Jonathan	Dressed in rags – her face hidden by a hood –
Lost girl	Please... help me.
Jonathan	And speaking so pitifully, her voice frail and weak –
Lost girl	I'm lost – I don't know where I am – what is this place?
Jonathan	She held her hand out towards me, imploring – a thin, white hand –
Lost girl	(*Holding out her hand to Jonathan*) You will help me? I'm so alone. So lost and alone. So cold, so hungry.

> *She moves closer to him.*

Jonathan	A hand more bone than flesh – and nails so long – like claws –

> The **lost girl's** voice suddenly becomes a savage snarl.

Lost girl	Lost and alone and cold and hungry!

> *She lunges forward at Jonathan, her hands like claws, as if to tear at him. He cries out and falls back. At that moment, **Dracula** enters.*

Dracula	No!

> The **lost girl** turns sharply, sees him, and hisses in fear. She cowers back from Jonathan as **Dracula** advances on her.

Dracula	Not him! Go! Be gone from here! Go, I say! Feed elsewhere tonight!

*Hissing and whimpering miserably, like an animal, the **lost girl** backs off and goes. **Dracula** turns and speaks to Jonathan.*

Dracula	Mr Harker? You are Mr Jonathan Harker, from England?
Jonathan	(*Still shaken and confused*) Yes…
Dracula	I am Count Dracula. I thought you might be lost and came to meet you. It was fortunate I did, I think. Are you all right?
Jonathan	Yes… just –
Dracula	Of course. You should not have left the road, Mr Harker. It was a mistake. In these parts, one should never leave the road. It is not wise.
Jonathan	That girl. Who is she?
Dracula	A girl. An orphan. She lives here in the mountains since her parents died. There was plague. Her mind is crazed. There is no real harm in her.
Jonathan	She seemed frightened of you.
Dracula	Yes.

There is a pause.

Dracula	Come, now, Mr Harker. Let us go back to the road. My home is not far. We have had a poor meeting. I will try to make it up to you. Some food and wine, and a good night's sleep and you will feel, I am sure, fully recovered after your… shock.

***Dracula** turns from Jonathan, moves a little way off and remains still, as **Jonathan** speaks to the audience.*

Jonathan	I followed him to the road, and then on to his home – a tall, imposing castle, built on top of a great crag. I didn't really take much of it in, then. I was tired, and still shaken after my... experience. But I felt better after I'd eaten, and thanked the Count, and said to him that I assumed we'd begin going through the documents the next day.

Dracula turns and speaks to Jonathan.

Dracula	Unfortunately, no. I have to be away during the day on business. I will not be here when you wake. But I shall take the documents with me, and we can go through them together when I return.
Jonathan	When will that be?
Dracula	In the evening.
Jonathan	I see.
Dracula	For tomorrow, my home is yours. There will be food prepared. Spend the day as you wish. I'm sure you will find many things here of interest. But please do confine your wanderings to the house. The chapel, in particular, is in a state of great disrepair, and is not at all safe.
Jonathan	Very well.
Dracula	May I have the documents?
Jonathan	Of course.

Jonathan hands the briefcase to Dracula.

Dracula	Thank you, Mr Harker. I shall begin studying them immediately. You must be tired. Your room is at the top of the stairs. I hope you find it comfortable. Goodnight.

Dracula turns and walks to the back of the stage. Jonathan speaks to the audience.

Jonathan	I slept fitfully and woke late to a fine, clear day. I found food waiting for me, ate, and then passed the time exploring the many rooms in the castle. But, almost from the moment of my

waking, I was increasingly aware of a... strangeness about the place... a sense of decay and death... a rottenness within its very stones. In every room and passage, I found evidence of a history that reached far back into the past – a history once grand and noble, perhaps, but degenerate now, wasted, caving in upon its own lifeless sterility.

> ***Dracula*** *turns and comes forward. He speaks to Jonathan.*

Dracula   My ancestors have lived here for many centuries. Long before the building of this castle they were a power in the land. A fierce, proud race, warrior-poets, defenders of their homeland against the forces of barbarism. They were true patriots, Mr Harker. They loved their country. They gave themselves to its rivers and forests and mountains, fed the very earth with their blood. And it grew rich and fertile with that blood. But now, the earth grows barren. The glories of the past crumble with the stones of this castle. The bones of my ancestors are dust in their tombs. I am the last of their line. In me alone they have life. And there are times I grow weary.

> ***Jonathan*** *speaks to the audience.*

Jonathan   It was the next evening. As the sun set the Count arrived. I ate the food he brought me – though he did not eat. And we talked in the great hall, by the light of a fire that cast crooked shadows across the cobwebbed walls.

Dracula	(*Continuing his explanation*) This is the reason I have made the decision to come to your country. There is nothing here for me now. Only the past. And one must look to the future, always.

Jonathan turns to Dracula.

Jonathan	Have you studied the documents?
Dracula	Yes. Everything appears to be in order.
Jonathan	And the property?
Dracula	It is excellent! I could desire none better.
Jonathan	There's nothing you wish to discuss?
Dracula	No. My good friend, Mr Hawkins, has been most thorough and meticulous. As, I'm sure, has been his assistant. He has written to me, and speaks of you highly.
Jonathan	It's very good of him. You're ready to sign, then?
Dracula	No. Not yet.
Jonathan	But you said everything was in order.
Dracula	Indeed it is.
Jonathan	Then may I ask the reason for your not signing?
Dracula	Yes. It is because I do not wish to. When I have completed all my preparations for leaving, then I will sign. It will be my last act here.
Jonathan	I see.
Dracula	Is it difficult?
Jonathan	I was rather hoping to have our business concluded tonight, and begin my journey home tomorrow.
Dracula	Then I am sorry to disappoint you. Is it so urgent you return?
Jonathan	Not urgent, but... desirable... to me.

Dracula   But it is desirable to me that you stay. For a few days only. I rarely have guests, Mr Harker, and it is a novelty of which I am loathe to be deprived. A few days, until my preparations are complete. Then you may go. Humour me in this, please. Say you will agree.

Jonathan   You appear to have left me no choice.

Dracula   Is it your heart that draws you home again, Mr Harker? Your heart and your loved one?

Jonathan   What?

Dracula   I found this among your papers.

He takes a photograph from his pocket and hands it to Jonathan.

Dracula   Your wife?

Jonathan   My fiancée…

Dracula   She is very beautiful. Such fine, strong features. There is a nobility about her, a strength and depth of character. She is proud, yes?

Jonathan   I wouldn't say proud –

Dracula   You are a lucky man. Do not be concerned. You shall see her again before long. Until then, remain my guest.

***Dracula** turns and goes. **Jonathan** speaks to the audience.*

Jonathan   I looked at the photograph of Mina, the woman who was to be my wife. And it was as if I was seeing her for the first time. Seeing her as he had seen her. There was something about the way he'd looked at her, a kind of… hunger in his eyes. And suddenly, I felt the great distance that lay between us, a distance that seemed to be drawing me away from her. And suddenly too, I was unaccountably afraid.

***Jonathan** goes.*

Scene 2

***Mina** enters and speaks to the audience.*

Mina   It was a few weeks after Jonathan left that I went to Whitby to stay with Lucy. We'd been friends since childhood, and had written to each other regularly since Lucy had gone to live there. I was so looking forward to seeing her. Especially as, since Jonathan's leaving, I had experienced an increasing sense of… unease and anxiety, which came to me in strange, disturbing dreams. Dreams I could not remember on waking… except that, in all of them, there was a shadow, a formless shadow that seemed to be reaching out towards me.

***Lucy** enters and speaks to Mina.*

Lucy   (*Laughing*) And since when have you paid any attention to dreams, Mina?

Mina   (*Turning to Lucy*) I don't, Lucy, not really...

Lucy   You poor thing. It's only that you're missing Jonathan.

Mina   Yes, I know.

Lucy   And it won't be long before he's home again, will it?

Mina   No...

Lucy	There you are, then. Dreams are nothing but… dreams. Nothing to be gloomy about.
Mina	Am I gloomy? I'm sorry, I don't mean to be. I'll try and be more cheerful.
Lucy	Good. Because I have some cheerful news. Some very cheerful news indeed.

Mina turns and speaks to the audience.

Mina	I'd known she had something to tell me ever since she met me at the station. Lucy was never very good at keeping her heart a secret. My… subdued manner had prevented her from telling me straightaway. But now that telling was to be delayed no longer.
Lucy	I wonder if you can guess?
Mina	(*Turning to Lucy*) I'd rather you told me.
Lucy	And I'd rather you guess. Can't you guess? Please. Look at me, Mina. Can't you?

*Mina looks hard at Lucy. Then she speaks
to the audience.*

Mina	Then I saw the truth of it. What it was that made her eyes shine so, that had deepened the colour in her face, that lent a brightness to her whole being – I saw what it was that she'd been bursting to tell me ever since she'd met me at the station. She'd had a proposal of marriage.
Lucy	No. You're wrong.
Mina	(*Back to Lucy*) Oh – I was sure –
Lucy	Not one proposal. Three!

Mina speaks again to the audience.

Mina	Of course, only Lucy could have had three proposals. And, of course, she could not rest, now, until she'd described each of her suitors in great detail.

Lucy	First of all, there's Doctor Seward. He would just do for you, Mina, if you weren't already engaged to Jonathan. Although he's only 29, he's in charge of a large asylum in the town. I only made his acquaintance a short while ago, and had no idea of the depth of his feelings for me, until he came to see me the other day.

*Dr John Seward enters in a flashback scene, and speaks to the audience as if he is speaking to Lucy. Throughout, **Lucy** speaks to Mina.*

Seward	Lucy – there's something I must speak to you about. I will come straight to the point – it concerns the manner in which... I have come to regard you...
Lucy	Poor man. He was trying to be so cool and composed, and yet I could tell how nervous he was. It quite made my heart ache for him.
Seward	Though I have known you but a brief while, Lucy, you have become dear to me – very dear. And I hope that I may also have become dear to you. So dear, in fact, that you might wish... to share your life with me.
Lucy	Of course, I told him that I could not. Not because of any ill-feeling towards him, but because my heart belonged to another.
Mina	Another?
Seward	Another? (*He holds up his hand as if to silence her*) There's no need to apologize. I understand. I'm sorry to have troubled you.
Lucy	Then he took my hands so tenderly in his and spoke with kindness and, I believe, complete sincerity.
Seward	(*Turning to Lucy*) I hope you will be happy with the man you have chosen. And if ever you find yourself in need of a friend, you must count on me as one of your best.

> *Seward turns, and walks to the back of the stage.* **Mina** *speaks to Lucy.*

Mina Poor Doctor Seward. Now, who is the second?

Lucy The second is a man with the delightful name of Quincey Morris.

> **Quincey Morris** *enters in another flashback scene and introduces himself. He has a slight American accent. Once again, he speaks to the audience as if he is speaking to Lucy, while* **Lucy** *speaks to Mina.*

Morris Quincey P. Morris.

Lucy He's an American – though he's lived so long in this country that he's lost all but a trace of his accent.

Morris A good friend of John Seward – and Arthur Holmwood, whom I believe you also know.

Lucy And on many evenings he amused us all with his stories and – tall tales.

Morris For I've travelled the world, Miss Lucy, and I've been in places and seen such things that folks here in safe little England would never even dream of.

Lucy But then, one of those evenings, being alone with me, he made his quite unexpected proposal.

Morris Travelled the world, I have, and there's nothing I like better – but I'd be willing to hang up my boots and settle for a warm fire in a little country house, if I thought I'd be sharing that fire and that house with the one who means most to me. I mean you, Lucy.

Lucy And, once again, I said that I couldn't accept such an offer, because my heart was given to someone else.

Mina Someone else again? Who is this someone else?

Lucy	Be patient. You'll hear.
Morris	(*Turning to Lucy*) Lucy, I have to tell you I'm disappointed. Mighty disappointed. I had thought the two of us – I thought we got on tolerably well – well enough in fact to… but it seems I was mistaken. But you've been honest with me, Lucy. Honest and direct, and I thank you for that. And though you might not have found a husband in me, you've found yourself a true friend, and one who'll never let you down, whatever kind of fix you're in. I thank you again, and take my leave.

> *Morris* turns and walks to the back of the stage.

Lucy	And he was gone, and he'd been so sweet that my heart felt like breaking, and I wept. I wept, Mina.
Mina	I'm sure you did, Lucy.
Lucy	And it was while I was still weeping that another man came into the room.

> *Arthur Holmwood* enters in a third flashback scene and again he speaks to the audience as if he is speaking to Lucy. **Lucy** continues to speak to Mina.

Holmwood	Lucy.
Lucy	Arthur Holmwood, only son of Lord Godalming. I've not told you of him before, Mina. I've not told you how from the moment we first met he won my heart. I had never told him how I felt. And until that night, he had never confessed any feeling to me.
Holmwood	But now I do. And I ask if you would do me the greatest honour, and become my wife.
Mina	And this time you said yes?
Lucy	This time I said yes.
Holmwood	And made me the happiest of men. (*He turns and speaks to Lucy*) I'm afraid I must leave you for a little while to return

home. My father is not well. But when he is better, and when I return, then we shall be married.

> ***Holmwood*** *turns and walks to the back of the stage.*

Mina   So, it's to be Arthur Holmwood, then.

Lucy   Yes. It could be no other. But Mina – Doctor Seward and Mr Morris are so… so sweet… and I do have some affection for them…

Mina   Of course you do.

Lucy   And though I do love Arthur… I sometimes wonder why it is a woman must choose only one man to be her husband –

Mina   Lucy!

Lucy   Have I shocked you, Mina? Do you think I'm wicked? I can't help what I think –

Mina   No. I don't think you're wicked. But I do think you should be satisfied with one husband – as I will be with Jonathan.

Lucy   Yes, you're right of course. (*Impulsively*) Perhaps we can make it a double wedding, Mina. Me and Arthur, and you and Jonathan, when he returns from abroad. That would crown my happiness. I'm sure I don't know what I've done to deserve such happiness. All I can do is to thank God for sending me such a husband, and such good, true and dear friends.

> ***Lucy*** *and* ***Mina*** *go.* ***Seward***, ***Morris*** *and* ***Holmwood*** *come forward and speak to the audience.*

Seward   But though we were good and true friends –

Morris   Though we kept her in our hearts and thoughts –

Holmwood   And loved her more than anything –

Seward   We were powerless to help her –

Morris   God was powerless to help her –

Holmwood   The time when the evil came.

> *Seward, Morris and Holmwood go.*

. . . .

Scene 3

> *Jonathan enters and speaks to the audience.*

Jonathan   The fear I had felt that night did not leave me. Although Count Dracula continued to treat me with courtesy, there was something in his manner that hinted at some dark purpose, some shadow in his voice beneath his words that filled me with increasing dread. And, as time passed, it came to me that I was being kept prisoner in his castle, though for what reason I could not guess. And then, one night, my fears took on form and shape and stood before me, and I saw them in their true horror.

> *He pauses, collecting himself, as if he has to face the terror he felt that night again.*
> *As **Jonathan** continues his story, three **hags** enter slowly. They are dressed in ragged robes, with hoods covering their faces. They take up positions on three sides of the stage.*

Jonathan   I woke suddenly. It was still dark. I couldn't tell the time. Neither late nor early. A kind of... 'no-time'... where all time had ceased. Bright moonlight flooded the room, transforming it. Everything sharper, clearer, yet somehow unreal. As if I had stepped through a mirror into a world utterly different. I noticed first a sweet, rich smell in the air, a sickly perfume that was almost visible. And then – voices. I heard voices singing, soft at first, but growing stronger, a song without words, so beautiful... so fearful... a song of longing and desire... and despair... And with the song there came a mist. It drifted about the room, and glowed with a pale light, and there were shadows in the mist, shadows which took shape and form, and stepped out of the mist and stood before me.

> *Jonathan* turns, and faces the three hags.
> *Their hands are claws. Their harsh voices*
> *have a hypnotic effect on Jonathan,*
> *paralysing him. As they speak, they close in*
> *on him.*

Hag 1   From black chasms we come.

Hag 2   From earth's deep, from hell's pit.

Hag 3   From night's throat we come.

Hag 1   Listen to us.

Hag 2   Be still.

Hag 3   Listen. Hear our voice.

Hag 1   It is the scratch of the rat in the dry tomb.

Hag 2   The scratch of the spider's leg over the floor.

Hag 3   The scratch of the bat's wing in the hollow cave.

Hag 1   Do not move.

Hag 2   Do not stir.

Hag 3   Be still. You cannot move.

Hag 1   We are the death that cannot die.

Hag 2   We are the heart that cannot beat.

Hag 3   We are the soul that cannot fly.

Hag 1   We are hunger.

Hag 2   We are all that hungers under the cold moon.

Hag 3   We are hunger and you are our prey.

Hag 1   And already you are dead.

Hag 2	Already we feed.
Hag 3	Claws tear, teeth rip.
Hag 1	We suck the hot blood from your veins.
Hag 2	We suck the rich life from your limbs.
Hag 3	We suck the last breath from your soul.
Hag 1	We are the children of the night.
Hag 2	The wolf's howl.
Hag 3	The owl's shriek.
Hag 1	We are hunger.
Hag 2	We are all the hungers under the cold moon.
Hag 3	We are hunger, and you are our prey.

*The **hags** have completely encircled Jonathan now, and are about to take hold of him when **Dracula** enters.*

Dracula   Leave him!

*The **hags** fall back from Jonathan.*

Dracula   How dare you touch him! This man is not for you. Do you hear me? Leave him, I say. He belongs to me.

Hag 1   What then for us?

Hag 2   Where do we feed?

Hag 3   Is there nothing for us?

Dracula   Feed where you will. The child in its cot. The old woman by her fire. The priest at his prayers. All are for your taking, except him.

Hag 1   You are our master.

Hag 2	You made us, we are yours.
Hag 3	(*Demanding eagerly*) A gift for your creatures!
Three hags	A gift! A gift!
Dracula	You think I would forget my children? Outside there is something. It lives. It kicks. Its life is young, its blood new-born. Go. Take it. Feast well.
Hag 1	A child!
Hag 2	A human child!
Hag 3	He gives us life.
Hag 1	He gives us blood.
Hag 2	Come, sisters. We go.
Hag 3	We go to feed.

> *The **hags** go. **Dracula** approaches Jonathan.*

Dracula	You think this is a dream, Mr Harker? A terrible dream from which you will wake? I tell you, it is no dream, and you shall not wake. Your world is the dream, this world the reality. The world of night, which I have made. And soon, very soon, that world will engulf you, and you shall dwell in its darkness forever. You – and she who has your heart. You belong to me, Mr Harker, and so does she. And I shall feed upon you both. You first, then her. And it is you, you who send me to her. You give her to me. Know this, Mr Harker. Know it – and despair.

> ***Dracula** goes. **Jonathan** speaks to the audience.*

Jonathan	I woke the next morning from horror into horror. The light of day brought with it no comfort. I was locked within my room, a captive, and prey to a… a monster that fed on human blood. My only hope lay in escape, and throughout that day, and the night that followed, I formulated a plan.

Jonathan I had deduced that the Count walked abroad only through the hours of darkness and that, if I were to attempt an escape, it must be while the sun shone. But the next morning, I saw a cart arrive, driven by four men. And these four men carried a number of heavy wooden boxes from the chapel and loaded them onto the cart. It was not until late afternoon that the cart finally left, and I knew that I must act immediately. So I climbed out of the window, and made my way along its ledge. Then, I crossed to the next ledge, and the next, and so on, until I stood above the chapel. From there I leaped down onto its roof. There was a hole in the roof, and looking down, I saw several coffins. I dropped down through the hole, and stood before one of them. The lid wasn't fixed down, but lay loose on top. I took hold of the lid, and lifted it away. And there, in the coffin, lay the Count! Neither dead nor alive, eyes open and glassy, lips red with blood. In terror and disgust I turned away. My only thought was to flee from that terrible place. To flee from the place of death and doom.

Jonathan goes.

Scene 4

Mina enters and speaks to the audience. As she speaks, Lucy enters and stands by her, followed by Mr Swales who sits down on the bench seat. Mr Swales speaks with a Yorkshire accent.

Mina   After a while, the letters from Jonathan stopped coming. One week passed, a second week, and I heard nothing from him. I told myself that he was in a remote part of the world, that his duties would occupy much of his time, that there were any number of reasons why I should not hear from him – yet I could not dispel the feeling of unease that grew daily within me. But I did my best to allay my fears, and to pass my time pleasantly with Lucy, who was happier than I'd ever known her. And she seemed happiest of all when we walked together in the churchyard behind the old abbey, which stood on a headland looking down upon the harbour, and out across the sea.

Lucy introduces Mina to Mr Swales.

Lucy   Mina, this is Mr Swales. Our town's oldest inhabitant, so they say.

Mr Swales   And how would you know my name and my age, miss?

Lucy   My mother's told me all about you. (*To Mina*) Mr Swales claims to be nearly a hundred years old.

Mina   Is that so, Mr Swales?

Mr Swales   I do claim it when folk ask – though you must never believe all you're told.

Lucy   He's known as something of an oracle, aren't you, Mr Swales?

Mr Swales   If you mean I've knocked around long enough to have seen summat of the world and its ways, I won't disagree with you.

Mina   Perhaps you could tell me something, then, Mr Swales. I have heard it said that, whenever a ship is lost at sea, a phantom bell tolls out in the harbour.

Mr Swales	Aye, I've heard it said as well. And no doubt you've also heard it said there's a ghost haunts the old abbey.
Mina	That's right, yes! The White Lady! She appears from time to time at one of the empty windows. So I've been told.
Lucy	Usually at dusk, and with a look of sorrow and loss on her face. They say she died for love.
Mina	A delightfully chilling tale.
Mr Swales	That's as maybe. I've also heard it said – and by men and women with more education than me – that come the Last Day the dead will rise up out of their graves, and be as they were in life. But I don't put no more credence to that, neither, nor any such children's fancies.
Lucy	Mr Swales! You're an unbeliever!
Mr Swales	Miss, I've been on this earth a good few years, and in that time I've travelled across most of it, man and boy, aboard fishers and whalers. And if I've learned owt, it's to believe only what I see with my own eyes – and even then to doubt it.
Mina	I bow to your superior experience, Mr Swales. But do you really not believe in anything beyond our mere mortal existence?
Mr Swales	Do I believe in ghosts and such like? No, miss, I don't. The dead are so much dust and mould. Take these that are buried in this churchyard here. I've come to sit in this place for more years than I care to remember, and I've not heard one of them so much as sneeze, let alone seen one get out of his grave and walk.

Mina turns and speaks to the audience.

Mina	So we passed the summer, and many times had occasion to talk with Mr Swales. And the last such occasion was that evening in August, before the night of the storm.
Lucy	I think the weather will break soon.

Mr Swales	Aye, it will that, miss. And break with a vengeance if I'm not mistook.
Mina	(*Turning back to Lucy and Mr Swales*) It will bring us some relief, I hope. These last days have been so hot and oppressive.
Mr Swales	Let's just hope that's all it brings, miss, and nowt else.
Lucy	What do you mean, Mr Swales?
Mr Swales	To be honest, I don't rightly know what I mean. Call it a feeling. There's summat coming with this storm. What it might be, I can't say. Though I sense there's nowt good about it.
Mina	This isn't like you, Mr Swales. You sound almost… superstitious.
Mr Swales	Maybe it's just that I can feel my own death approaching.
Lucy	Surely not! You're hale and hearty yet!
Mr Swales	I've walked this earth a long time, miss, and I can't be expected to walk it forever.
Mina	I refuse to believe it, Mr Swales. You'll live to be a hundred, I'm sure.
Mr Swales	Maybe, and maybe not. Who can tell when death will come to us? Maybe it's when we're looking for it, and maybe it's not. But whenever it comes, and whatever form it takes, I pray I may meet it grinning.

Mina turns and speaks to the audience.

Mina	We left him there, on his seat, and returned to Lucy's home. And I wish I'd turned round and looked upon him once more, and raised my hand in farewell, for after that evening, I never saw him in the world again.

Mina and Lucy go. Mr Swales speaks to the audience.

Mr Swales   I watched them go, and there were more I wanted to say to them, but I couldn't find the words. I wanted to warn them, but I didn't know of what. Bolt your doors, seal your windows tight, for there's summat coming, out there over the North Sea, riding high and proud on the back of the storm, something wicked in the wind and the shivering light. And though I can't see its face, it smells like death. Aye, I should've told those things, but I didn't, and never had the chance again. For that night I saw its face, and they found me the next day with my neck broke and my heart burst. So evil came into this land, and cast its shadow upon it, and took possession.

The lights fade to blackout.

· ·

Act 2
· · · · · · · ·

Scene 1

*The lights rise. The **newspaper reporter**
enters and speaks to the audience.*

Reporter Yesterday's sudden and violent storm was perhaps the most
ferocious to have erupted on the town within living memory.
This fact alone would warrant its inclusion in this newspaper.
Yet it also brought with it events so strange and unique that they
will be imprinted on the town's memory for a long time to come.
The most noteworthy of these was the appearance of a ship at
the height of the storm, with all sails set, making for the harbour,
and caught in the very teeth of the gale. Despite the howling
winds and driving rain, many townsfolk gathered at the harbour
side to watch with baited breath and anxious hearts as the ship
was tossed this way and that on the heaving ocean, several times
disappearing completely from sight beneath the onslaught of the
waves, only to reappear again, to the cheers of the gathered
crowd. Against all apparent odds, the ship weathered the storm,
and at last drew into the harbour, where the townsfolk prepared
to greet and congratulate the gallant crew – until it was
discovered that but for one man, there was no crew aboard – and
that one was a corpse tied to the ship's wheel. A great awe came
on all as they realized that the ship had found harbour unsteered
save by the hand of a dead man!

*The **coastguard** enters and speaks to the
audience.*

Coastguard

As coastguard, I was first on board the vessel. She was Russian, a merchantman. Her name, the *Demeter*. What became of her crew, God alone will ever know. As for the poor fellow at the ship's wheel, some desperate need must have driven him to lash himself there. The rope had cut through his flesh to the bone, and there was a crucifix clutched in his right hand. The doctor later confirmed that he'd been dead for two days, but could find no definite cause of death – except perhaps fear. For there was a look on his face of... sheer terror and horror... a look, I confess, that chilled me to the bone. As for the ship's cargo, all I found in the hold were several wooden boxes, about six feet in length, and these contained nothing but mouldering earth. The whole thing is a mystery, and a damned unpleasant one at that, and as far as I can tell shall probably remain so.

*The **coastguard** goes. The **reporter** also turns to leave, then stops and turns back to the audience.*

Reporter

There was one more unusual event worthy of mention in this journal. Shortly after the ship came into harbour, a large, grey dog was seen by many, including this reporter, to leap off the deck onto the quayside, and then to make its way along the path to the clifftop where the churchyard stands. But what the dog was doing on board the ship, and what became of it thereafter no one knows, for to date it has not been seen again.

*The **reporter** goes.*

. . . .

Scene 2

*Immediately, **Renfield**, a patient at Dr Seward's asylum, enters. He looks unkempt and seems agitated. He cries out, wildly.*

Renfield

My master! My master has come! He is here! Master! Hear me! I'm waiting! I'm ready to do your bidding, Master!

***Bennett** and **Withers** enter. They are attendants at the asylum. **Bennett** carries a cudgel.*

Bennett	What's all this noise about, Renfield?
Withers	Keep it down.

Renfield turns to them.

Renfield	He's here. At last! He's come with the storm! He summoned it and it brought him!
Bennett	Who are you talking about?
Renfield	My master.
Withers	Oh, yes? And who might your master be, Renfield?
Bennett	Old Nick, most likely.
Withers	Or Old King Cole.
Renfield	I've waited for him a long time. I have been faithful. He knows I have. And he will reward me for my faithfulness.
Bennett	You're going to get a reward, are you?
Renfield	Oh, yes. He promised I would.
Withers	And what might that reward be?
Renfield	Life. Eternal life.
Bennett	His master must be God Almighty, then.
Withers	Or like I said, the Devil.

Renfield starts to chant.

Renfield	Life is blood and blood is life. Life is blood and blood is life. Life is blood and blood is life...

*He continues chanting as **Bennett** and **Withers** speak.*

Bennett	There he goes again.

Withers	Shut it, will you, Renfield?
Renfield	Life is blood and blood is life, life is blood and blood is life...
Bennett	Gets on my nerves, that does.
Withers	Mine, too. That's enough, I said!

> ***Renfield's** chanting grows louder and more agitated.*

Renfield	Life is blood and blood is life; life is blood and blood is life; life is blood and blood is life...
Bennett	Give us a break from it!
Withers	Shut it or I'll shut it for you!

> ***Renfield** cries out and attacks **Withers**, scratching his face.*

Renfield	Life is blood!

> ***Withers** cries out.*

Bennett	You –

> ***Bennett** hits **Renfield** with the cudgel, knocking him down. At that moment, **Seward** enters.*

Seward	What's going on? Bennett! Stop that!
Bennett	He attacked Withers, Doctor Seward.
Withers	Scratched my face with those nails of his. Look! He's drawn blood.
Bennett	Went wild, he did.
Seward	Even so, I've told you before we are not to use violence against our patients.
Withers	Even if they use violence against us?

Seward	That is what marks the difference between them and us, Mr Withers.

Renfield squats on the floor, sucking and licking his fingers. Seward approaches him.

Seward	He appears calm enough, now.
Bennett	Don't let that fool you, Doctor Seward. There's murder in his heart, sure enough. Cut all our throats if he could.
Seward	Renfield. Renfield. What are you doing?
Renfield	Blood. Life is blood.
Withers	Oh, God. He's licking my blood off his fingers.
Bennett	He's an animal. That's what he is.
Seward	No, Mr Bennett. He's not. I'm afraid he's all too human, and that's the tragedy of it. You can both go, now. I'll stay with him for a while.
Withers	You be careful, Doctor Seward. This storm's got him all wound up. He's drawn blood, and given the chance he's likely to do it again.
Seward	I'll take care.
Bennett	We won't be far if you need us.

Withers and Bennett go. Renfield remains squatting on the floor. Seward speaks to the audience.

Seward	After my disappointment in the matter concerning Miss Lucy Westenra – soon to become Mrs Lucy Holmwood – I devoted myself even more entirely to my work here at the asylum. I became intrigued by the case of one particular patient – Renfield. His madness showed itself in a most singular obsession, which I discovered some time ago, upon one of my first visits to him.

The following action takes place in flashback.

*Renfield begins to move about the floor, as if hunting something. Then, he reaches out suddenly, and snatches something up, cupping it in his fist, and hugging it to himself with pleasure. **Seward** turns to him.*

Seward   Renfield. What's that you have there?

Renfield   You can't have it! It's mine!

Seward   I don't want it, whatever it is. I simply want to know what it is. Show me, would you?

*A little suspiciously, **Renfield** stands and crosses to Seward.*

Renfield   Careful. It mustn't escape.

He holds his cupped fist up to Seward's face and then opens it a little.

Seward   A fly!

***Renfield** closes his fist again.*

Renfield   One of many. Many. There shall be many.

*He moves away from **Seward** who continues to tell his story to the audience. As **Seward** speaks, **Renfield** takes a small box out of his pocket, and places the caught fly in it.*

Seward   He requested sugar to lay in small piles about his cell, which he used to attract the flies, and also a small box in which to keep them. I saw no reason to deny his requests. Indeed, I was eager for him to continue in his obsession, in order that I should observe it, and see in what direction it might lead.

***Renfield** turns to Seward, holding up the box.*

Renfield   You hear them? Buzzing, buzzing. Fat flies, filled with life. The box is full. It can take no more.

Seward   What will you do with them?

Renfield   You'll see. Wait! Hold this! Don't let them out!

> *Renfield gives the box to Seward, drops to his knees, and hunts again. Once more, he makes a grab at something, and cups it in his fist. He stands, triumphant, and turns to Seward.*

Renfield   There! Now we can move on!

Seward   What's that? Another fly?

Renfield   No. It isn't flies I want, now. It's spiders. I have a spider! And he shall feast well, and grow fat!

> *Renfield takes the box from Seward, and places the spider in it.*

Renfield   One spider, and another, and another. Soon, no more flies, and a box full of spiders. Fat spiders. Do you see?

> *He turns from Seward, drops to the floor, and begins hunting spiders, snatching them up and placing them in the box. **Seward** speaks again to the audience.*

Seward   Needless to say, I did not. But daily I observed him gripped in the mania of this new obsession – as eager almost as he was to follow it through to its ultimate end.

Renfield   Life is blood and blood is life.

Seward   (*Turning to Renfield*) What? What's that you say?

Renfield   Life is blood and blood is life. Spiders eat flies and birds eat spiders. And here's a whole boxful! A boxful of spiders for a bird to feed on. And he will grow so fat, so fat and full of blood and life.

> *He turns from Seward and sits on the floor with his back to the audience. **Seward** turns back to the audience and continues his story.*

Seward	So at last I began to glimpse some reason and progression in his mania. From spiders he moved on to birds, luring several sparrows from outside into his room.

Bennett and Withers enter.

Bennett	And a right mess they've made of it as well.
Withers	Filth and droppings everywhere.
Bennett	You sure it's healthy to let him keep them in here, Doctor Seward?
Seward	I don't think there's any harm in it. They aren't that much of a nuisance at present. And it will be interesting to see what he intends to do with them.
Withers	I know what I'd like to do with them. Get rid of the whole lot and clean this place up. Clean him up as well, while I'm at it.
Seward	I'm sure it won't continue for much longer, Mr Withers. I've been observing each obsession of his and –
Bennett	(*Suddenly noticing Renfield*) Oh, my God! You animal! You filthy, stinking animal!

> As **Bennett** cries out, **Renfield** scuttles
> away, stuffing something into his mouth with
> his hands.

Seward	Mr Bennett! What is it? What's wrong?
Bennett	Him! That's what's wrong! You see what he's doing? He's eating one of them blessed birds! Didn't even kill it! Just stuffed it into his mouth and he's eating it alive and raw!
Withers	No harm, eh, Doctor Seward? If you ask me, there's nothing but harm in that one. He's a creature full of harm and wickedness, if I've seen it in any living soul.
Bennett	Best get this place cleared of these birds, Doctor Seward. If you don't, he'll soon have it cleared for us.

Bennett and Withers go. Renfield sits, rocking himself backward and forward, and muttering over and over to himself. Seward speaks to the audience.

Seward   After we took the birds away – to which he made most violent objection – he sank into a morbid, depressed state, uncommunicative except for his repeating over and over of his almost prayer-like chant.

Renfield   Life is blood and blood is life, life is blood and blood is life, life is blood and blood is life, life is blood –

Renfield stops suddenly and looks up. Seward continues to speak to the audience.

Seward   Until the night of the storm.

Renfield   He's here. My master! He has come!

Seward   The night of madness and horror.

Renfield   He brings me freedom! He brings me life.

Seward   The night when evil came.

Seward goes. Renfield stands, walks to the front and speaks to the audience.

Renfield   My master has come in the belly of the storm. My master is here, and he brings me blood!

Renfield goes.

. . . .

Scene 3

Mina enters and speaks to the audience.

Mina

The storm came but brought no break in the weather. The days that followed were hot and oppressive, almost unbearable. And with that oppressiveness, my concern for Jonathan's welfare increased. But not only for him. Since the storm, Lucy had become restless and distracted. She slept badly, and told me of strange, unsettling dreams that seemed to sap her energy. And she feared the coming of night, she said. She feared these dreams that haunted her. I thought that perhaps it was the terrible death of poor Mr Swales that had affected her. But then, one night, I saw that this was not so.

*During the following, **Lucy** enters behind Mina. She wears a shawl around her shoulders, held together by a brooch. She sits on the bench.*

Mina

I awoke myself from some dream to find Lucy's bed empty. The large window that faced out onto the garden was open. I rose and went out. There was dew on the grass, and I could see her footprints, leading across the garden and out. I followed them, and they led towards the ruins of the abbey. And there, in the distance, I saw her, on the bench where Mr Swales used to sit. But there was something strange about her. It was as if she was… waiting for something… or someone.

> *As **Mina** speaks, **Dracula** enters and crosses to Lucy. He stands over her. His face is hidden from the audience. **Lucy** raises her head towards him.*

Mina What I saw next, made me think that I was still sleeping, still in the grip of some terrible dream. Out of the shadows a figure approached her, stood over her, and she raised her head towards him as if in greeting. The figure stooped over her, and she was lost in the darkness of his shadow. And I knew it was no dream, that it was real, for I gave a cry, and the figure turned its head towards me. In the light of the full moon, I saw its face. And it was the face of a beast.

> *__Dracula__ turns suddenly to the audience. He is wearing the horrific mask of a wolf. He turns from Lucy and takes a step towards Mina. Then **Lucy** gives a sudden cry.*

Lucy No!

> *__Dracula__ stops, turns back towards Lucy, then goes, quickly. **Mina** goes to **Lucy**, who looks at her, as if waking from a dream.*

Lucy Mina? What's happening? What am I doing out here?

Mina It's all right, Lucy. You've been sleepwalking, that's all.

Lucy Sleepwalking?

Mina Yes. I woke and found your bed empty. I followed you here.

Lucy I've had the strangest dream... so strange... but I can't remember it...

Mina You're shivering. It's cold. Let me wrap your shawl more closely round you.

> *__Mina__ readjusts Lucy's shawl around her shoulders and neck, fastening it with the brooch. As she does, **Lucy** gives a little cry of pain.*

Mina	I'm sorry. I must have caught your neck with the pin. There. No harm done.
Lucy	Mina. I'm frightened.
Mina	Frightened? Of what?
Lucy	I don't know –
Mina	Don't be. I'm here. There's nothing to be frightened of. Nothing at all.

Mrs Westenra enters and speaks to the audience. As she does so, **Mina** *sits with Lucy, holding her hand, stroking her hair, comforting her.*

Mrs Westenra	In the days that followed, my daughter grew increasingly lethargic. I, of course, was much concerned for her welfare, but hoped that, with the care and attention of Mina and myself, she would soon recover her full health.
Mina	(*To the audience*) But she didn't. With each passing day, the energy and life seemed to be draining out of her body. Yet at night she could not sleep. Several times I woke to find her sitting up in bed, staring wildly about her, as if disturbed by some presence I could not perceive.
Lucy	A face at the window, red eyes gleaming. Something scratching at the glass. It wants to get in!
Mrs Westenra	(*Approaching Lucy*) It's only a dream, dear. Pay no heed to it. Dreams can't harm you.

Mrs Westenra speaks to Mina.

Mrs Westenra	It is only a dream, isn't it?
Mina	(*Disconcerted*) Of course. What else could it be?
Mrs Westenra	I don't know. I'm sure I don't know.

Mina   (*To the audience*) I told her nothing of what I'd seen that night in the churchyard. What could I tell her? For I hardly knew what it was myself.

Mrs Westenra   (*Turning back to the audience*) I wrote to Mr Holmwood and told him of Lucy's condition, and he replied by return of post to say that he would be with us within the week. I felt sure that his arrival would do something to revive Lucy.

> **Dracula** *enters and stands at the side of the stage.* **Lucy** *looks up suddenly and points towards him.*

Lucy   (*Softly and urgently*) There! The same! The same face, the same red eyes!

> **Mina** *continue to tell her story to the audience.*

Mina   We were sitting together in the churchyard one evening, when suddenly she spoke, her voice low and urgent.

Lucy   Do you see him, Mina? There!

Mina   I turned and saw the figure of a man, standing some way off. But the setting sun was behind him, and I could not see his face.

Lucy   Always the same.

Mina   (*Turning back to Lucy*) What do you mean, Lucy? Who is that man? Do you know him?

Lucy   No. At least... I don't know what I mean... it was like my dream... the dream I have every night...

> **Dracula** *goes.*

Mina   Don't think of your dreams, Lucy. Think of the life you have. Think of Arthur. He'll be here soon, and then everything will be all right.

Mrs Westenra   (*To the audience*) And I was glad that he was coming. Being... not well myself, I don't know how I would have cared for Lucy alone. Because shortly after, Mina told us she would have to leave.

> *Mina stands and speaks to Lucy and her mother.*

Mina   I've had news of Jonathan. A letter came today... from a hospital in Budapest. That's where he is. He's been ill, but he's recovering now. That's why I haven't heard from him these past weeks.

Mrs Westenra   Ill? Do they say in the letter what's wrong with him?

Mina   Not exactly. He appears to have had... some kind of breakdown...

Lucy   Oh, Mina!

Mina   You do see, don't you? I must go.

Mrs Westenra   Yes, Mina, of course you must.

Lucy   Jonathan needs you. Go to him. I'll be all right. Arthur will be here in a day or two. And, thanks to your care and your dear friendship, I am feeling much better. By the time you return, you'll see I'll be quite my old self again.

Mina   I'm certain you will, Lucy.

Lucy   You can depend upon it.

> *Mina speaks to the audience.*

Mina   So I said farewell to Lucy, and left, eager to make the journey, but full of fear and apprehension as to what I might find at the end of it. I did not know that my journey was to be much longer than I thought, that it would take me to a world I did not know existed. And that what I found there would be like nothing I could ever imagine.

Mina goes. Mrs Westenra sits beside Lucy on the bench. Holmwood, Morris, and Seward enter and stand separately on three areas of the stage, around Lucy and her mother, as if protecting them. They speak to the audience.

Holmwood   And we could not imagine –

Morris   No one could ever imagine –

Seward   When we came to stay with her –

Holmwood   To love and protect her –

Morris   To be her guardians as we'd promised –

Seward   We could not imagine what world it was –

Holmwood   What world of shadow had fallen across ours –

Morris   And it had called to Lucy –

Seward   And she had entered it.

. . . .

Scene 4

Professor Van Helsing enters and stands at the centre front of the stage. He speaks only to the audience.

Van Helsing   I was abroad when my former student, Doctor Seward, wrote to me concerning the girl's case. And though it intrigued me and I gave it my full attention, yet I did not fully realize the grave danger she was in. I wrote to him, suggesting certain courses of action that could be taken and, to be honest, put the matter to the back of my mind.

During the following, Holmwood, Morris and Seward speak to the audience.

Holmwood   But despite these remedies, Lucy did not get better.

Morris   Her condition only seemed to grow worse.

Seward   And she grew weaker and paler every day, as if something
                        were draining the blood from her body.

>   *Lucy* speaks to the audience, her voice flat,
>   as in a dream.

Lucy   I lived my life between waking and dreaming, not knowing
                        which was which, as if my soul were slowly being drawn from
                        my body. My days were a mist that thickened about me, my
                        nights were filled with fear that came with the scratching of
                        claws at the glass. And once there was a sweetness in the room
                        and the fear turned away, but then the sweetness was taken
                        and the fear returned, and it was stronger than ever.

Van Helsing   The second letter I received from Doctor Seward informed me
                        in more detail of her symptoms, the foremost of which was an
                        extreme anaemia, with accompanying lethargy. Doctor
                        Seward's concern for his patient was obvious and, while I
                        could offer no explanation, I wrote back and suggested that
                        she be given, without delay, a transfusion of blood, in an
                        attempt to reverse, or at least arrest the illness.

Holmwood   But nothing worked. Nothing! No treatment or remedy!

Morris   It seemed we were all powerless to help her.

Seward   And the only outward sign of any infection, the two wounds
                        on her neck that would not heal.

Van Helsing   (*Realizing the truth*) A wound to her neck! It was then, and
                        only then, that the true nature of this 'illness' became clear to
                        me. And the peril in which the girl's life and soul stood. I
                        wrote back immediately, saying that I would come there
                        myself. In the meantime, her room was to be hung with
                        flowers of wild garlic – the door and windows especially – and
                        that these should on no account be moved. I would explain all,
                        I said, when I arrived.

>   *Van Helsing* goes.

Holmwood	Flowers of garlic? Is this medical science or peasant superstition?

Holmwood turns his back to Lucy.

Morris	Despite our doubts we did as Professor Van Helsing had instructed.

Morris turns his back to Lucy.

Seward	Because, quite frankly, I was at a loss, and there seemed nothing else that we could do.

Seward turns his back to Lucy. **Holmwood, Morris** and **Seward** remain in their positions throughout the following. **Lucy** speaks to herself as if in a dream. As she does so, she moves to draw back the curtain to reveal the French window. She remains there, gazing outside.

Lucy	Nothing they can do. Nothing to be done. See, the sun sets, the sky grows red, the earth grows dark. And out of the darkness and the redness in the west he comes, a mist creeping along the earth, cold fingers reaching towards my heart. Squeezing it, squeezing it tight. There, he stands at the window. There he waits to gain entrance. The same, always the same.

Mrs Westenra speaks to Lucy.

Mrs Westenra	What was that you said, Lucy?
Lucy	(*Coming out of her dream*) What, Mother? Did I speak?
Mrs Westenra	Yes.
Lucy	I don't know what I said. I don't remember. Nothing of importance.
Mrs Westenra	It's growing dark. Come away from the window, now. Get into bed.

Lucy moves back to sit on the bench, but continues to look towards the window.

Lucy   Not just yet. I want to sit here for a while and watch the sun
                           set. It's so beautiful, isn't it, Mother?

Mrs Westenra   The sunset?

Lucy   The world, Mother. The world is so beautiful. I wish the dark
                           wouldn't come to take it from us.

Mrs Westenra   The world is still there in the dark. It's only the light that's
                           gone. Go to sleep. Then the light will return all the sooner.

Lucy   No, it won't. I fear the light will never come again.

Mrs Westenra   Lucy! What do you mean?

Lucy   (*Turning back to her mother*) Nothing.

Mrs Westenra   You make me afraid when you speak like that.

Lucy   I'm sorry. I'm just tired. I don't know what I'm saying.

Mrs Westenra   (*Caring and concerned*) Get into bed then –

Lucy   (*Sharply*) No! (*She softens her voice*) I will, soon. When the sun
                           has set. You can leave me. I'll be quite all right.

Mrs Westenra   If you're sure –

Lucy   Go and sit with Arthur. Keep him company.

Mrs Westenra   He has company. Have you forgotten? Doctor Seward and Mr
                           Morris are both here.

Lucy   Yes, of course. My three guardians. I'm very lucky, aren't I,
                           Mother?

Mrs Westenra   Yes. You are. And I'm very lucky to have such a daughter as
                           you.

Lucy   Kiss me goodnight.

> *Mrs Westenra kisses Lucy. Lucy holds her
> suddenly, very tight, then lets her go.*

Lucy	Mother, when you see Arthur, will you tell him that I love him very much?
Mrs Westenra	You can tell him that yourself. Do you want him to come and see you?
Lucy	No. Please. Just tell him.
Mrs Westenra	All right. I will.
Lucy	Thank you. Goodnight now, Mother.
Mrs Westenra	Goodnight, dear.

> *Mrs Westenra goes. **Lucy** speaks to the audience.*

Lucy	I turned back to look out of the window. The sun had almost set. A line of darkness was rising up into the sky from the horizon, deepening, spreading. And in the dark, a knot of blackness forming, hardening, tightening, my death approaching. Coming like a ship on a blood-red sea, a ship with ragged, tattered sails, riding the waves of darkness. And a figure on the prow, leaning towards me, hungry and eager, urging the ship on. Then the waves rolled higher and higher, and they crashed about me, and all was drowned and my death was here.

> *Dracula enters through the French window, leaving it slightly open.*

Dracula	Lucy. I have come for you at last.

> *Lucy stands in fear. **Dracula** holds out his hand to her.*

Dracula	Come to me. Come willingly. You know you must.
Lucy	Where's my mother? I want my mother!
Dracula	She will not come. I showed her my face and it was too much. She's dead. Gone to hell with all her sins upon her.
Lucy	No!

Dracula   Why should you care about the dead? The dead mean nothing to such as you or I. They are so much dust and mould. We tower above them. We stride the world like giants. We are immortal. Soon you will know the taste of pure freedom, and there is none so sweet. One kiss. One last kiss is all.

> *Dracula walks towards Lucy, takes her hand, leans towards her and kisses her once, gently, on the neck. He steps back and lets go of her hand.*

Dracula   There. It is done.

> *He turns to go.*

Lucy   Where are you going?

Dracula   I must leave you now. But only for a little while. Not long, and you shall be with me.

> *Dracula goes. Lucy speaks to the audience.*

Lucy   And he was gone, but the darkness remained. And my soul wept but I did not hear it, for soon I too would walk in the dark world eternal.

> *Lucy goes.*

. . . .

Scene 5

> *Holmwood draws the curtain to cover the French window and then returns to his place. Van Helsing enters and speaks to the audience.*

Van Helsing   So I came at last to a house of sorrow and mourning. But though I had failed the poor girl in her struggle with horror, yet I knew there was still work to be done. For I may have come too late to save her life, but not perhaps too late to save her soul.

Seward, Morris and Holmwood turn to Van Helsing. Seward introduces Van Helsing to his two friends.

Seward	Arthur – Quincey – this is the man I told you of – Professor Van Helsing.
Van Helsing	I am pleased to meet you both – though I wish the circumstances had been happier.
Morris	So do we, Professor. And none more so than Arthur here.
Van Helsing	Mr Holmwood – you were to have married the unfortunate young lady. My sincere condolences to you.
Holmwood	Thank you. I wish – I wish you could have arrived sooner –
Van Helsing	So do I.
Holmwood	Perhaps you might have been able to save her.
Van Helsing	Perhaps – and perhaps not. You were with her when she... finally passed away?
Morris	We all were.
Van Helsing	Tell me what happened.
Holmwood	What is there to tell? She died.
Van Helsing	Yes, but... if you could describe in detail the circumstances of her final moments...
Morris	(*Angry and upset*) What the hell for? What good would it do?
Van Helsing	It may help to prevent others from succumbing to the same... illness.
Seward	You think it may be something contagious?
Van Helsing	It may be. I cannot tell unless I have all the facts before me. Please.

Holmwood   I went in to see her early in the morning. She was lying on the floor and the window was open –

Van Helsing   Open? I gave instructions that it was to be kept shut at all times, especially during the night –

Seward   The window had been closed. I checked it myself before I went to bed.

Van Helsing   What of the garlic flowers I said should be hung from it?

Seward   Mrs Westenra removed them. The smell –

Van Helsing   That was a bad mistake.

Morris   If it was, Mrs Westenra paid a heavy price for it.

Van Helsing   Yes. She died as well. From heart failure, you said, John?

Seward   That's right. I found her in her own bedroom. The window was open there too.

Van Helsing   I see. Mr Holmwood, if you can find it in yourself to continue…

Holmwood   I put Lucy back into bed. I could see she was very weak. Her breathing was so shallow –

Van Helsing   Did she say anything?

Holmwood   No.

Van Helsing   Nothing?

Morris   She did try to speak. Just before the end –

Van Helsing   Did you hear what she said?

Morris   No. Her voice was too weak. Is it important?

Van Helsing   It may have been. Was her end peaceful?

Holmwood   (*Interrupting*) Yes, yes it was. Very peaceful. She passed as gently from this world, as she had lived in it.

Van Helsing	I am… glad to hear it. And the marks on her neck? John, you wrote to me of two small wounds on her neck. Caused by the pin of a brooch, you said.
Seward	That's right. They weren't particularly serious – but they wouldn't heal.
Van Helsing	And were they still open when she died?
Seward	No. They appeared to have healed up entirely. In fact, there was no sign of them.
Van Helsing	And her features in death, they were peaceful?
Holmwood	I've already told you.
Van Helsing	May I see her?
Morris	She's in her coffin.
Van Helsing	Just for a moment.
Morris	It's been sealed.
Van Helsing	Nevertheless –
Holmwood	(*Very upset*) No! No, you may not see her! All these questions you're asking, what do they matter? What does any of this matter? She's dead! Nothing you can do will bring her back! Let her go to her rest. Let her be disturbed no more!

Holmwood storms out.

Van Helsing	He's understandably upset.
Morris	We all are, Professor.
Van Helsing	Of course, of course. Forgive my briskness, Mr Morris. It is not my intention to cause undue distress to the bereaved. However – (*He stops*) No. We will talk no more. As Mr Holmwood said, let Miss Westenra be interred, and be at peace. And let us all pray for her soul.
Morris	I'll say amen to that.

Morris turns to go, then stops, and turns
back.

Morris	One thing, Professor. When Arthur said she died peacefully – well... that wasn't quite the case.
Van Helsing	No?
Morris	Just before she died – at the moment of her death – something happened – a... change came over her.
Van Helsing	What kind of change?
Morris	Something in her face – a light in her eyes – something... savage – as if she had suddenly become possessed.
Van Helsing	And then?
Morris	Then it passed, as quickly as it came, and she died.
Van Helsing	Thank you for telling me, Mr Morris.
Morris	I thought I should. If it can shed any light on the cause of her death –
Van Helsing	It may shed a great light indeed.
Morris	Good. Because I told that girl I'd do anything for her, and even though she's gone from us, that still stands.

Morris goes. Van Helsing speaks to
Seward.

Van Helsing	John. What do you think killed her?
Seward	I confess I'm not certain. Loss of blood was certainly a factor.
Van Helsing	This continued throughout her illness, despite the transfusions you gave her?
Seward	Yes. It was baffling. A mystery.
Van Helsing	There is much that is mysterious about this business. And there is much that I fear may yet be revealed.

Seward　　What do you mean?

Van Helsing　　John, once the funeral is over, you and I shall go and talk together, in private. There are things I must tell you, things I have discovered, which I believe have a direct bearing on what has happened here. And if I am correct, we may still have work to do before the poor soul of Miss Westenra can finally be laid to rest.

Seward　　(*Horrified*) What do you mean?

Van Helsing　　Now is not the time. We shall talk later. Let us go and join the others.

Van Helsing and Seward go.

. . . .

Scene 6

*The **reporter** enters and speaks to the audience.*

Reporter　　There have occurred in recent days in the town, several incidents of children going missing from their homes. Three cases have so far been reported, and, in each case, the circumstances were strikingly similar. First of all, the three children all live in the same area of the town – that which lies close to the old abbey and the churchyard beyond. Second, while each child was happily missing for a period of one night only, and was discovered again the next morning, they were all found to be extremely weak and having a pale, almost emaciated appearance. And, in each case, the child spoke of being met by a young, beautiful woman, and taken by her for a walk. But none of the children can remember anything that happened after that, until the time they were recovered. Finally, and perhaps most disturbingly, on the neck of each child was a small wound, which appeared to have been inflicted by some wild animal. The public can rest assured that this newspaper will continue to report and investigate any further occurrences of these strange and unsettling events.

*The **reporter** goes. A **child** enters on one side of the stage and speaks to the audience.*

Child   I was playing with my friends by the abbey. They went home when it started to get dark, but I stayed a bit longer because I like watching the fishing boats come in. After I'd watched them I turned round to go home, and that's when I saw the lady.

Lucy enters on the opposite side of the stage and stands, watching the child.

Child   She was standing there, looking at me, and when I saw her she smiled and spoke to me.

Lucy   (*To the child*) Do you want to go for a walk?

Child   (*To Lucy*) It's getting dark.

Lucy   You're not afraid of the dark, are you?

Child   No...

Lucy   Then come for a walk with me.

Child   (*To the audience*) She was very beautiful and she had a nice voice, and she walked towards me and held out her hand.

Lucy   (*Approaching the child, holding out her hand*) I don't like walking alone. Come and keep me company.

Child   (*To Lucy*) Where will we go?

Lucy   Not far. Just for a walk. A little walk. Come. Take my hand.

*The **child** takes Lucy's hand, then turns to speak to the audience.*

Child   So I did, and she took me through the abbey and into the churchyard. And while we were walking she kept singing to herself. Only I can't remember what the song was. And I can't remember anything else either. I can't remember anything else at all.

***Lucy** and the **child** make their way to the seat.*

Lucy   Here we are.

Child   Where?

Lucy   Here. I like it here, don't you? Among the dead. It's so peaceful.

Child   It's dark –

Lucy   Yes. I like the dark. Don't you like the dark?

Child   I ought to go home now –

Lucy   Why? Why do you want to go home? Don't go home. Stay with me. I'm lonely. I have no friends. Will you be my friend? Stay here with me and be my friend. You can sleep here, here on this bench. Sit down. Sit down here, and I'll put my arm around you and sing to you, and you can sleep. Sleep and dream such lovely dreams.

*The **child** sits. **Lucy** sits next to him. She puts her arm around the child and sings, softly and gently. The **child** begins to fall asleep. On the far side of the stage, **Van Helsing** and **Seward** enter, watching secretly. **Van Helsing** carries a crucifix which he keeps hidden. They speak softly.*

Van Helsing There! You see?

Seward   It's her... Lucy...

Van Helsing	No. What you see is not Lucy. It is Nosferatu. The undead. You know now that what I told you is true.
Seward	Yes.
Van Helsing	Now! We must act quickly before she preys on this child.

> *The **child** is asleep now. **Lucy** stands and lays him down gently. Then she bends over him, as if she intends to do him some harm. **Van Helsing** runs forward, crying out, and brandishing a crucifix.*

Van Helsing	Back! Back, evil one! Leave him!

> ***Lucy** turns, savagely, and snarls and hisses like an animal at Van Helsing. She makes a threatening move towards him.*

Van Helsing	Back, I say! Leave this place! Away to your tomb!

> *He thrusts the crucifix forwards. As if in pain, **Lucy** backs offstage, snarling and hissing. **Van Helsing** lowers the crucifix.*

Van Helsing	John. See to the child.

> ***Seward** wakes the child.*

Child	(*Confused*) No – I want to go –
Seward	It's all right.
Child	Where's the lady?
Seward	She's gone. I'm a friend. There's nothing to be afraid of.
Van Helsing	(*To Seward*) I'll come to you later, at the asylum. Bring Mr Holmwood and Mr Morris there. It is time they too learned of this, and what it is we must do about it.
Seward	Very well. (*To the child*) How do you feel?
Child	Sleepy. What's been happening? I can't remember –

Seward	Don't worry. It doesn't matter. Come with me, now. I'll take you home.

> *Seward and the child go. Van Helsing remains onstage.*

. . . .

Scene 7

> *Van Helsing speaks to the audience.*

Van Helsing	I placed the crucifix at the entrance to the tomb, so keeping the creature from leaving and claiming more victims that night. Then, as we had arranged, I met with the others, and told them, as I had earlier told Doctor Seward, what I had learned myself over many years of that terrible creature of darkness and blood – the vampire.

> *Morris enters and speaks to the audience.*

Morris	He told us how, from ancient times, there had been tales of those that lived on after death. Creatures of the dark whose souls were lost, whose existence was a death-in-life.

> *Holmwood enters and speaks to the audience.*

Holmwood	How these undead could take on both human and animal form, and were, and are, known by many and varied names – the werewolf, the zombie, Nosferatu, the vampire.
Van Helsing	Having no soul, they have no humanity; they are beasts in human dress, driven only by appetite.
Morris	And that appetite is for human blood. They feed on the blood of the living. Blood sustains them and drives them. It is their only desire.
Holmwood	During the day they sleep in their graves and their tombs, for to be touched by the sun's light is fatal to them. The night is their time and it's then they walk the earth, immortal, seeking their victims in the hours of darkness.

Van Helsing   And once having found a victim, they prey on them, draining the blood from their body, and with each feeding their power over the victim grows. Until at last, death comes. But no ordinary death. For the power of the vampire has entered the victim's body, and they too become undead and immortal, and rise from their graves to feed upon others in turn.

Morris   And this, he said, is what had happened to Lucy.

Holmwood   Lucy had been the victim of a vampire.

Morris   And she, in turn, had become a vampire.

Holmwood   But I didn't believe it! I wouldn't!

Morris   Fairy tales! Horror stories!

Holmwood   How can we in our world believe such things?

> *Seward* enters and speaks to the audience. He carries a small carpet bag.

Seward   And then I told them what I had seen that very night. How I had seen Lucy walking – or the monster that inhabited Lucy's body. I told them how, for all my belief in science and the powers of reason, I had been forced, through the evidence of my rational senses, to admit the existence of another power, and that there were such shadows in our world.

> *Van Helsing* turns and speaks to the three men.

Van Helsing   Shadows, indeed, my friends. For while we may inhabit a world of light, there is also a world of darkness. Older than ours, perhaps, and often hidden from our more... enlightened eyes. But now that world has revealed itself to us, it has come upon ours, taken form and shape. And the form it walks in, at this present moment, is that of Miss Lucy Westenra. And we must act, act like heroes, with courage and strength, to drive it back to from where it came.

> *Seward* hands Van Helsing the carpet bag.

Van Helsing   (*To Seward*) Is everything here as I instructed?

Seward   Yes.

Van Helsing   Then we are ready. And, with the coming of night, we must act.

                    Morris and Holmwood speak to the audience.

Morris   But still we found it hard to believe.

Holmwood   Even as we went that evening to Lucy's tomb, I refused to believe it.

Morris   As we stood there, waiting, as the sun set, I could accept nothing of what we'd been told.

Holmwood   Until the light died, and the shadows deepened, and the thing of darkness came walking from the tomb.

                    Lucy, as a vampire, enters talking to herself.

Lucy   I am hungry. Last night I did not feed. Something held me, a power, terrible. Now it is gone and I am free and I will feed.

Morris   My God! It is her!

Van Helsing   As I said. The dead do walk.

Seward   I thought you'd sealed her in.

Van Helsing   Last night I did. Today I removed the crucifix.

Seward   But why?

Van Helsing   So they could see what she has become.

Lucy   (*She looks towards the men*) I see them. Four. Three I know, one I do not. Waiting for me. I sense harm. But what can they do? What is their power against mine? Weak, frail they are. But with blood. Hot with blood.

Seward   She's seen us.

Morris   What do we do, Professor?

Van Helsing	Wait, for the moment. Let her come to us.
Lucy	(*Still talking to herself*) He is there. I see him looking. He sees her, his dearest one. With him I shall begin. His love shall deliver him to me.
Van Helsing	Whatever she does or says, do not approach her. She is hungry, and very dangerous.

> ***Lucy*** *speaks, lovingly, to Holmwood.*

Lucy	Arthur? Arthur, is it you?
Holmwood	Lucy –
Van Helsing	Take care, Mr Holmwood.
Lucy	Arthur, my love. You have come for me at last.
Holmwood	Is it you?
Lucy	Yes. It is I, your own Lucy, your own true love.
Van Helsing	(*To Holmwood*) She is cunning. Do not be deceived by her.
Lucy	Come to me, Arthur. I'm not dead. I'm alive. You can see I am alive. Come. Hold me. I've been waiting for you, waiting for you to come to me.

> ***Lucy*** *holds out her arms to Holmwood. He is drawn to her, almost against his will.*

Van Helsing	(*Reaching out to restrain him*) No, Mr Holmwood! Don't go to her!
Holmwood	Leave me –
Seward	It's not Lucy. It's a monster –

> ***Seward*** *takes hold of Holmwood to hold him back.* ***Holmwood*** *flings him off.*

Holmwood	Let me go!

*As **Lucy** speaks, **Holmwood** moves slowly towards her.*

Lucy That's right, Arthur. Come to me. Don't listen to them. They tell you lies. You can see it's me, your own, your very own. Come to me, now, and we shall never be parted again, we shall be together for all time!

***Holmwood** is now within reach of Lucy. He holds out his arms to her.*

Holmwood Lucy –

*With an animal snarl **Lucy** lunges at him, grabbing his wrists, pulling him with force and fury to her. **Holmwood** cries out in sudden fear. At the same moment, **Van Helsing** drops the carpet bag and springs forward, taking the crucifix from his pocket. He too grabs at **Holmwood** and pulls him from her grip.*

Van Helsing (*To Lucy*) No, hell-hound! You shall not have him!

***Lucy** turns on Van Helsing.*

Lucy You, then!

***Van Helsing** thrusts the crucifix forward against Lucy's face. She screams in pain and terror, as if being horribly burned. She staggers back, clutching at her face. **Van Helsing** walks towards her, the crucifix held up, forcing her back with it, as she rages and snarls. **Lucy** goes, still snarling. **Van Helsing** lowers the crucifix.*

Morris Arthur? Are you OK?

Holmwood Yes. Thank you. (*To Seward*) John, forgive me for how I acted.

Seward There's nothing to forgive.

Holmwood Professor –

Van Helsing	Say nothing, Mr Holmwood. You were severely tested tonight. And I think that now you must be tested even further.
Holmwood	In what way?
Van Helsing	You loved Lucy, did you not?
Holmwood	I still love her.
Van Helsing	Then help her to find peace. Free her soul from the monstrous shackles that bind it. Kill the beast within her. Do you have the strength of heart to do this?
Holmwood	I think so. I pray so.
Van Helsing	Good. (*He picks up the carpet bag*) Here I have the weapons of mercy. Let us go into the tomb, and do what must be done.

*They all freeze except for **Holmwood**, who steps forward and speaks to the audience.*

Holmwood We entered the tomb. She was lying in her coffin. As I approached, I saw her eyes open, saw the savage light that flashed in them, the ferocious and pitiless hunger. She strove to rise but could not, pinned down by the power of the cross. I knew now this was not Lucy. It was some evil thing that had fed on Lucy, and would feed on others, and go on feeding unless it was destroyed. I steeled myself to the task. I took up the weapons of mercy. I commended myself to God, and drove the wooden stake into her heart.

*From offstage a sudden, loud, monstrous scream is heard, rising, then dying away to silence. **Morris**, **Seward** and **Van Helsing** speak to the audience.*

Morris The beast howled in rage and pain, then fled into the darkness.

Seward And she lay still and I could see by her face that she was at peace.

Van Helsing And it was done. But it was not over.

The lights fade to blackout.

Act 3
· · · · · · · ·

Scene 1

> *The lights rise.* **Mina** *enters and speaks to the audience.*

Mina The hospital in Budapest where I found Jonathan was run by a religious order who cared for the sick. He had been found wandering on the outskirts of the city. Apart from exhaustion, there was nothing physically wrong with him. But mentally… his mind had suffered some terrible shock that had left it almost broken. What had caused this shock the sisters could not tell, and I did not wish to know, not until he was recovered and ready to speak of it. So I nursed him back to health, and there in Budapest we were married, and then began our journey back to England.

> ***Jonathan*** *enters and speaks to the audience.*

Jonathan And it was on that return voyage, that at last I found the courage, and the strength, to tell Mina all that I had experienced. But even then, I hesitated, for fear that she would not believe me, would think me mad… for fear that, perhaps, I *was* mad…

Mina And indeed, when he first told me… I did not know what to think. I could not bring myself to believe that such evil existed in our world. It was only when I learned that Lucy – and her mother – were dead, that I began to perceive some possible connection.

> ***Van Helsing*** *enters and speaks to the audience.*

Van Helsing So they travelled to Whitby and met with Mr Holmwood and Doctor Seward, who told them the circumstances surrounding the girl's death. And at Doctor Seward's suggestion, they met with me, and I too heard Mr Harker's story.

Mina

Poor Jonathan. When he spoke of his ordeal, when he described the terrible things he had suffered, I could see how the horror of it lived in him again. I knew the pain it caused him, I felt that pain myself, and would have saved him from it if I could. But instead I urged him on, for I knew it was vital to us all, that his story must be told to the end.

Jonathan turns and speaks to Van Helsing.

Jonathan

I could not have done so without Mina. It was she who gave me the strength…

Van Helsing

It was good that you found such strength, Mr Harker. Your wife's instincts were correct. I believe there is a connection between your experiences, and her friend's death. A very strong connection. (*To Mina*) What your husband has told me – and what you yourself have told of Lucy's illness – they explain much. Things begin to fall into place, and the mystery is not so obscure.

Mina

You believe it was Count Dracula who killed Lucy?

Van Helsing

I am almost certain of it. But before we can be sure, there are more facts we have to ascertain. What did Doctor Seward tell you of Lucy's death?

Mina

Not everything, I'm certain. Mr Holmwood was with us, and I think he was afraid of distressing him.

Van Helsing

Speak to Doctor Seward again. Ask him to tell you everything. You will find it distressing. But I think too you will understand more about this business. Mr Harker, I would like you to see what you can find out about Carfax Manor, and if anyone has taken residence there in recent times.

Jonathan

Of course.

Van Helsing

I myself must go to London. There is a man I know of who is an expert in European genealogies. I hope from him to find out more about this Count Dracula. I shall return by tomorrow evening. Then we shall all meet, and lay out the facts before us. And then we may be able to see how we are to act in the face of this danger. A danger that I believe is among us, and threatens us all.

> *Jonathan* and *Van Helsing* go, separately.
> *Mina* speaks to the audience.

Mina Although we were staying with Doctor Seward, I had to wait until he had finished his morning duties before I could speak with him. Then he told me of Lucy's death – and of what happened after it…

> *Mina* falters in her speech, obviously upset by what she has learned, but she continues, attempting to overcome her distress. As she speaks, *Seward* enters and approaches her.

Mina To think of her as I'd always known her – as I saw her last – of her dying like that – that was bad enough – but to think of what she had become – having to endure a second death – I was silent when he told me – I said nothing – there was nothing to be said – I could not say how I felt – I did not know what I should feel – and then – for a moment – I saw – the world that she had entered – the dark world where she had walked – for a moment, it opened up before me –

> *Seward* speaks to Mina.

Seward Mrs Harker –

> *Mina* turns to him, as if coming out of a trance.

Mina Doctor Seward – I'm sorry –

Seward Yes, I understand…

Mina You were speaking of someone –

Seward A patient here – Renfield. I believe that he too, in some way, may be connected with this.

Mina Tell me of him.

Seward I can do more than that. If you wish it, if you feel able, you may see him –

Mina   I do wish it. Yes. Yes, I will.

Mina and Seward go.

. . . .

Scene 2

Renfield enters, alone, carrying his box. He looks around nervously, then squats on the floor, opens the box, and begins to eat greedily what is inside, cramming it into his mouth. When he has finished, he looks in the box, turns it upside down, shakes it, then drops it on the floor. Then he looks up, as if at some sound, or the awareness of a presence.

Renfield   Is this all? No more?

Renfield stands and he speaks out, as if to some unseen presence.

Renfield   No more for me? Flies. Spiders. You send them to me, yes. Drifting in on golden rays of light. A little sustenance. Your gift to me, so gracious. But not enough. They're not... enough! You promised more. Rats, you said, you would bring. Meat, blood. Blood is life. I waited. I still wait. I have been faithful. And this is all!

He picks up the box and holds it up.

Renfield   You and I, we are of the same kind. You understand. You know my desire. There should be more, more for me, there should be more than this!

Bennett and Withers enter behind Renfield.

Bennett   Renfield!

>*Renfield* starts at his name but he does not
>turn round. He holds the box to his chest,
>hiding it, draws himself upright and
>composes himself, staring outwards.

Bennett   You hear me, Renfield? There's a little surprise in store for you.

Withers   A very nice surprise. You're going to have a visitor.

Bennett   And not just any visitor, Renfield. A visitor of the female variety.

Withers   A woman. A young woman.

Bennett   Friend of Doctor Seward's, or something. And she's asked to have a look round the place.

Withers   She asked to see you. God knows why she should want to, mind.

Bennett   Are you listening, Renfield? You've got a visitor. Did you hear?

>*Renfield* continues to keep his back to
>Withers and Bennett as he speaks.

Renfield   Yes. I heard. Any friend of the good Doctor Seward is a friend of mine. She will be made more than welcome.

Withers   Going to serve her tea and cake, are you?

Renfield   Sadly, such simple, civilized amenities are not made available to me here.

Bennett   What are you doing there, Renfield? Why don't you turn round? What are you looking at out of the window?

Renfield   The evening. It's beautiful, don't you think?

Withers   It's like any other evening.

Renfield	No, it's not. Look at the colour of the sky. That deep autumn blue. This is the best time of all, I think. The turning of the year. Summer's passing, and the world rolls incessantly towards winter. And here we stand, at the cusp, held in balance between the two. Life and death co-existent. At such times, and in such light, is the heart of the world illuminated.

Renfield quotes from a poem.

Renfield	'To see a world in a grain of sand, And a Heaven in a wild flower, Hold infinity in the palm of your hand, And eternity in an hour.'
Bennett	What are you going on about, Renfield?
Renfield	Blake.
Withers	What?
Renfield	William Blake.
Bennett	Who's he when he's at home?
Withers	A mate of yours?
Renfield	A poet. I was quoting one of his poems.
Bennett	Quoting poetry, now, are you?
Renfield	I didn't expect you to have heard of him.
Withers	You expected right.
Renfield	He saw the world as it truly was. The shining world that exists beneath this world of shadows. The eternal, everlasting world. Angels and devils. Heaven and hell. From the struggle between these two, life draws its raw energy.
Bennett	You know what, Renfield? What you said just then? I didn't understand a blessed word of it!
Withers	Load of nonsense, if you ask me.

Renfield	They said Blake was mad, too.
Bennett	Mad, was he? But did he eat flies?
Withers	And spiders? Did he eat spiders, Renfield?
Bennett	I bet he didn't. That's your speciality, isn't it?
Renfield	It may have been that once I... entertained such a notion. That by the consumption of living creatures, one could extend one's own life. Perhaps indefinitely. But that, I know now, was a delusion. A psychosis, of which I have been cured.
Withers	Cured, are you?
Renfield	I have applied to Doctor Seward for release.
Bennett	Oh, yes, we know all about that, don't we?
Withers	We do. And I'll tell you what else we know. You ain't going to get it.
Bennett	Doctor Seward'll never release you, Renfield. And do you know why? (*To Withers*) Tell him why.
Withers	'Cos you're a looney. That's why. You're stark raving mad.
Renfield	(*Quoting*) 'I am but mad north-north-west; when the wind is southerly, I know a hawk from a handsaw.' Shakespeare. Surely even you have heard of him.
Bennett	What's your game?
Renfield	Game?
Bennett	What are you up to, eh?
Renfield	I don't understand –

Withers and *Bennett* approach Renfield.

Withers	Yes, you do. You're up to something. All this fancy talk, trying to pretend you're better. What is it, eh? What's going on in that nasty little head of yours?

Renfield   I'm sure I don't know what you mean –

> *Renfield turns to them. They see the box.*

Bennett   Don't you, then? Cured, are you? So what's this? (*Indicating the box*) Still up to your old tricks?

Withers   What's in it? Flies, or spiders?

Bennett   Or something bigger?

> *Renfield opens the box and shows it to them.*

Renfield   It's empty. You see?

Withers   You won't need it any more, then, will you?

Renfield   What?

Bennett   Seeing as you're cured.

Withers   Might as well give it up.

> *Withers holds his hand out for the box. Renfield's composure begins to crack a little, and he makes to draw the box away from Withers. But Withers snatches it from him and puts it in his pocket. At that moment, Seward and Mina enter.*

Seward   Renfield. I'd like you to meet someone.

> *Renfield turns from Withers and Bennett to Seward and Mina. He reacts to Mina.*

Renfield   I was told I was to have a visitor. But I didn't realize... it would be one so... exquisite.

> *He approaches Mina.*

Renfield   Madam. I am more than honoured to welcome you to my... humble abode.

He bows.

Mina Thank you, Mr Renfield.

Renfield I only wish I could offer you more suitable hospitality. But, as you can see –

Mina It's no matter.

Renfield Ah, but it does, it does matter. To me. However, I have great hopes of soon being released from this place, back into the world. And then, perhaps, we may meet under more comfortable circumstances.

Mina (*To Seward*) Is that so, Doctor Seward? Is Mr Renfield to be released?

Seward He has asked me to consider the matter. And... I am considering it.

Renfield I hope not too long, Doctor.

Seward We shall have to wait and see.

Renfield I bow to your judgement, of course. (*To Mina*) Madam, you have the advantage of me.

Mina In what way, Mr Renfield?

Renfield In that you know my name, but I do not know yours.

Mina Forgive me. I should have introduced myself. I am Mrs Harker.

Renfield starts visibly at the name.

Renfield Harker? Mrs Harker, did you say?

Mina Yes –

Seward What's the matter, Renfield?

During the following, Renfield begins to grow agitated.

Renfield	Your husband is... Jonathan Harker?
Mina	That's right! Do you know him?
Renfield	Yes... no... I've heard of him... I had some business once with his employer... in the days when... before I came here...
Mina	Mr Hawkins – ?
Renfield	Yes... that's the man... he... mentioned your husband's name to me...
Mina	Favourably, I hope.
Renfield	What?
Mina	I said –
Renfield	(*Growing more anxious and agitated*) You're his wife, then. Mrs Harker. Mrs Jonathan Harker.
Bennett	I should watch him, Doctor Seward.
Withers	Looks like he's heading for one of his turns again.
Seward	Yes. Perhaps we should –
Renfield	And you're here! You've come here!
Mina	Mr Renfield –
Renfield	In this place! Here! Now!
Seward	(*To Mina*) I think we ought to leave –
Renfield	(*Urgently and intensely*) Yes! Oh, yes! You ought to leave! Certainly you ought to leave!
Seward	He sometimes gets distressed like this... and he can become violent –
Renfield	But you won't. No. You won't leave. He won't let you.
Mina	What do you mean?

Bennett	He don't mean anything.
Withers	It's all just his ravings.
Seward	Come, Mrs Harker –
Renfield	Because you're beautiful... so beautiful... even more than she was... your skin so soft –

> *Renfield* *puts out a hand to touch Mina's face. She cries out and draws back.* *Bennett* *and* *Withers* *grab hold of him roughly.*

Bennett	That's enough of that!
Withers	Didn't take you long, did it?
Mina	No! Don't! Don't hurt him! Poor man! He can't help himself. Can't you see how wretched he is?

> *Bennett* *and* *Withers* *let go of Renfield. He stares at Mina, in shock at her kind words.*

Renfield	I am. I am… wretched. I am in hell.
Seward	(*To Mina*) We should go, now.
Mina	Yes. I've seen enough.

> *Seward* *and* *Mina* *go.* *Bennett* *and* *Withers* *approach Renfield again.*

Bennett	Cured, then, are you?
Withers	Ready to go back into the world?
Bennett	You know what, Renfield? Somehow I don't think so.
Withers	'Cos you're a nasty little piece of work. That's what you are.
Renfield	Oh, yes. Thoroughly nasty.
Bennett	And that's why you're here.

Withers   And that's why you're going to stay here. Forever.

Renfield   Not just me, though. All of us. All nasty pieces of work. You
                       and I. No difference between us. All beasts with our snouts in
                       the trough –

Bennett hits Renfield.

Bennett   Speak for yourself.

Withers hits Renfield.

Withers   You're the beast, not us.

Bennett hits Renfield again.

Bennett   The lowest kind of beast.

*Withers hits **Renfield** again. **Renfield**
falls to his knees, clutching his stomach and
gasping.*

Withers   So, just you remember that.

*Bennett and **Withers** turn to go. **Withers**
stops and turns back.*

Withers   Here, Renfield. You'll need this.

*He takes the box from his pocket and drops it
in front of Renfield. **Withers** and **Bennett**
go. **Renfield** remains still for a while,
attempting to recover. Then he shudders. All
pretence at his being 'cured' has now gone.
Almost against his will, he picks up the box,
grimacing, as if it is hateful and monstrous to
him. Then, in a sudden, impulsive act of rage
and frustration at what he is, he crushes the
box, crying out as he does so.*

Renfield   No!

> *He drops the crushed box on the floor and sits still. He remains onstage throughout the following scene.*

Scene 3

> *Mrs Outhwaite and Jonathan enter, on another part of the stage. **Mrs Outhwaite** is talking to Jonathan as she enters. She speaks with a Yorkshire accent.*

Mrs Outhwaite   You want to know about Carfax Manor, do you? Well, I'm the person to tell you, if there's anybody can. Though it's not a subject I'm too fond of these days.

Jonathan   You're caretaker there, aren't you?

Mrs Outhwaite   That's right. Been caretaker there these past ten years. Though if you want the job, you're welcome to it. I've done with the place. I'm resigning my position as from tomorrow, even though I'll feel the want of the money. For while there may be many things money will buy, I've never known it buy peace of mind. And I haven't had peace of mind there these last two months or so. Neither peace of mind nor spirit. What is it you want to know?

Jonathan   I'm interested in a delivery that may have been made there recently – a delivery of... goods, round about the beginning of August.

Mrs Outhwaite   And what might you be wanting to know about that for?

Jonathan   I'm a lawyer. The whereabouts of these goods are of some legal importance.

Mrs Outhwaite   I'll tell you, then. It's with the delivery of them... goods that all my troubles began. Goods, you call them. Boxes, I call them. Wooden boxes full of God knows what. The very day them boxes were delivered, that's the day I stopped having peace of mind and spirit.

Jonathan   These boxes. Do you know where they came from?

Mrs Outhwaite   Off that ship. That ship that came in with the storm. You might've known there were summat funny about them, coming off a ship that were steered by a dead man. You know about that, do you?

Jonathan   Yes... I had heard something...

Mrs Outhwaite   It were Alf Tranter had the delivery of them. Six of them, there were. He brought them up on his cart, and it took him and his three lads to shift each one of them into the house. Right heavy, they were. I asked him what were in them, and do you know what he said to me? 'Mould,' he said. 'They're full of mould. Like summat's gone and died in them.' And it were from the minute them boxes were put in the old place that things started turning queer.

Jonathan   In what way?

Mrs Outhwaite   Noises, for one.

Jonathan   Noises?

Mrs Outhwaite   That's right, sir. Noises. Now, I know old houses make noises, and when you've worked in a place you get to know them. They're kind of friendly, if you take my meaning. But these noises, they're summat different altogether.

Jonathan   How are they... different?

Mrs Outhwaite   Unholy. That's how I call them. Unholy and unwholesome. Whisperings. Murmurings. Scratchings. Like something with claws scratching and scraping its way along the floors. First time I heard it, I were in there giving the place a bit of an airing, and I were standing just by the cellar door, and up it comes from down below. That scratching and scraping. Sent me cold, it did. And that weren't the last time I heard it, either. And always from the same place.

Jonathan   The cellar?

Mrs Outhwaite   That's right. The cellar. Where me and Alf Tranter put them boxes. But it weren't just noises. It takes more than a few unwholesome noises to put the wind up a woman like me.

Jonathan   What else?

Mrs Outhwaite   Rats, sir. The place is full of them. There's always been a few rats there, of course. Can't help it, an old place like that, and it's been empty for nigh on a century. But it's more than just a few I'm talking about. There's a whole multitude of them. And big, bigger than any natural rat has a right to be. I came upon one of them just a week or so back, perched atop of the stairs, and looking down at me. Well, I weren't going to be outfaced by no rat, so I went up them stairs waving my broom at it, but the blessed thing just stood there staring at me with them red eyes and big yellow teeth. And I'm not ashamed to say I backed off from it, sir. But I'll tell you this about it. I had a good look at it when I were on the stairs, and there were blood on its mouth. Fresh blood. And where that blood came from don't bear the thinking about.

Jonathan   Have you ever seen any human figure about the house?

Mrs Outhwaite   I can't say that I have, no. I've not seen nobody. Though sometimes I've had a kind of sense of somebody being there. Like I were being watched. But the only thing I've ever seen is them rats. And another creature.

Jonathan   What kind of creature?

Mrs Outhwaite	Well, now, when that ship come in out of the storm, it were all in the newspaper as how there were summat else on board, apart from the dead man. A dog, they said it were. A big dog that came jumping up out the hold and ran off into the town. They said nobody saw it again after that, nor knew what had become of it. But somebody did. Somebody saw it. I did. And it weren't no dog.
Jonathan	What was it?
Mrs Outhwaite	I only caught sight of it the once. In the wood that grows at the back of the house. It were getting dark, but I saw it there, coming out of the trees. It stopped when it saw me, and looked me full in the face before it turned round and went back into the wood. I've only seen summat like it once before, years ago, when I were a young woman and went down to London and paid a visit to the zoo. But I'll swear on any Bible you like that this creature were the same as I'd seen there. It were a wolf.
Jonathan	A wolf?
Mrs Outhwaite	I don't care if you don't believe me –
Jonathan	I do believe you, Mrs Outhwaite. And you have been most helpful. Thank you. Please, take this for your trouble.

He gives her some money.

Mrs Outhwaite	I won't refuse you. I'll be in need of a bit of brass now I've decided to quit that place. It'll be in short supply. But I'll have something I don't have now. Peace of mind, sir. Peace of mind and spirit.

*Mrs Outhwaite and Jonathan go,
separately.*

· ·

Scene 4

*Renfield looks up and stands, suddenly,
aware and alert. He speaks aloud to himself,
with a mixture of fear and anticipation.*

Renfield	Night comes. The dark. And with it... the thing of the dark. Shadows fall, a mist gathers, creeps along the ground. See! He comes! And all hell's creatures with him.

> *Renfield quotes from 'Hamlet'. As he speaks, **Dracula** enters behind him.*

Renfield	'Tis now the very witching time of night, When churchyards yawn, and hell itself breathes out Contagion to this world. Now could I drink hot blood – '

> ***Renfield** breaks off, aware of Dracula's presence.*

Renfield	No more. Words fail me. He's here.
Dracula	Yes. I am here.
Renfield	Master.
Dracula	Won't you turn and look at me?
Renfield	Yes, Master.

> ***Renfield** turns to face Dracula.*

Dracula	There is fear in your eyes.
Renfield	Of course –

> ***Dracula** approaches Renfield.*

Dracula	And something else. Something other than fear –
Renfield	Master! She was here. I have seen her!
Dracula	Yes. I know. I feel her presence. Her warmth. Her scent fills the air. You spoke with her?
Renfield	Yes!
Dracula	I too shall speak with her soon. She will hear my voice. And then she will hear no other.

Renfield	She will be yours.
Dracula	Mine, yes. And no one this time shall take her back.
Renfield	And for me?
Dracula	For you?
Renfield	What for me?
Dracula	Do you not like what I send you?
Renfield	Spiders, flies, birds –
Dracula	It is life.
Renfield	But not enough. Small, mean lives –
Dracula	So is your life small and mean. This is what you are.
Renfield	I am of your kind –
Dracula	No! You are not of my kind! You shall never be! You are – as you are. Be content with it.
Renfield	No!

> *Suddenly, **Dracula** grabs Renfield by the throat.*

Dracula	No? You would say no to me! You would dare! You know how I could crush you, little man. Crush you out of all existence, like one of those insects you feed upon. It would mean nothing to me. You live because I choose you to live. And if I choose you to die – you die.

> *He squeezes Renfield's throat, choking him. Then, he throws him down to the floor. **Renfield** gasps.*

Dracula	There. I choose you to live – for now. And I give you something. Your freedom.
Renfield	Freedom?

Dracula	To leave this place. Your attendants sleep. The door to your cell is open. Your path is clear. Go.

> *Renfield now realizes that Dracula has abandoned him. He speaks in despair.*

Renfield	Go? Go where? Where would I go? What is there for me out there?
Dracula	The same as here. Nothing. I have done with you, Renfield. For a while you... amused me. Now I put you from me. But for the small services you have done, I make you this gift. Your life.
Renfield	It is no life!
Dracula	Then die. That too may be a gift .

> *Dracula approaches Renfield.*

Renfield	No – no –

> *Renfield scurries in fear offstage. **Dracula** turns from him and speaks aloud to himself.*

Dracula	She sleeps here tonight. For safety, she thinks. I hear her breathing, soft. I hear the delicate rustle of her skin, her hair. I hear the whispering of her most secret dreams, dreams she hardly even hears herself. But she will know them. For they call to me.

> *Dracula goes.*

. . . .

Scene 5

Van Helsing enters and speaks to the audience.

Van Helsing This is what I have learned of Count Dracula. These are the few facts I have gathered, and this is what I told the others when I returned. He has been known in the East for many centuries. First, as a warrior of noble race, who fought for his homeland against the Turk. A man of courage, great intelligence, strength, and iron will. And merciless in his dealings with the enemy. Merciless and cruel. And a man of whom it was whispered, even then, that he had dealings with the Evil One. A pact was made, perhaps. His soul for the immortality of life. Or simply the will was so strong that even death could not subdue it. Whatever the cause, he passed from natural life to life unnatural, from being mortal man to Nosferatu. The undead. Wampyr. Vampire. So he has lived on, through the centuries, feeding upon the blood of the living, making of them others of his kind. But all these are lesser beings than he. For though he has long ago shed the last of his humanity, though he has become monster, yet that will, that intellect, that merciless intelligence lives on, and, like him, they have grown strong in power. Strong and terrible. And he reigns alone, supreme.

*Seward, Holmwood, Morris, Jonathan, and **Mina** enter on their lines and speak to the audience. **Mina** wears a lace shawl.*

Seward This is the enemy that has come among us.

Holmwood This is the corruption that dwells in our midst.

Morris The darkness that has taken root in our hearts.

Jonathan The darkness that must be destroyed.

Mina For if not it will surely grow, and spread until it has consumed us all.

Van Helsing turns and speaks to them.

Van Helsing	Yes, indeed. And this is why we are met here together. To see what means are at our disposal for our battle against the foe. For the danger is imminent, and we must act with all urgency.
Seward	Even more urgency now that Renfield has escaped.
Jonathan	He's still at large?
Morris	Arthur and I have been helping to search for him all day. It's as if he's just vanished from the face of the earth.
Van Helsing	No. He will be near, but hidden. He is slave to Dracula. He will not be able to go far from his master. But he is of little account to us at the moment. It is on the master that we must fix our attention.
Holmwood	I think there's one thing that should be done first.
Van Helsing	What's that?
Holmwood	From what Jonathan has told us, Mina is the most immediately vulnerable. Isn't that so?
Jonathan	Yes.
Holmwood	Then it would be best to remove her from that danger. She should leave now, and return to London.
Van Helsing	Well, Mrs Harker? What do you say to that?
Mina	I appreciate your concern for my welfare, Arthur. But I am determined to play my part in destroying this monster. I shall not go. I shall stay.
Holmwood	(*To Mina*) I saw what happened to Lucy. If the same were to happen to you –
Mina	I'm quite resolved. I shall not be... packed off to London. I shall remain here, where I may do some good.
Van Helsing	Bravely spoken, Mrs Harker. Your courage and determination shall be an example to us all. And we shall all need those qualities if we are to have any hope of succeeding in our plan.

Morris   Do we have a plan?

Van Helsing   What we have learned about the nature of the beast shall help us to form one. We know, for example, that the vampire rises only at night. During the day he must rest. And he must rest in his native earth. That is the reason the boxes were brought here. They are his sanctuary from the sun, which is deadly to him.

Jonathan   And we know where those boxes are. And if we can prevent him from returning to them –

Seward   (*Interrupting*) Wouldn't it be simpler to deal with him as we dealt with – ?

Holmwood   You can say it, John. As we dealt with Lucy. Yes, those are my thoughts exactly.

Van Helsing   We may yet have to. But not now. It is too late. In a short time the sun will be setting. We could not reach Carfax Manor in time to take him at his rest. He will be rising soon, going about his business. But, while he is away, we shall strike our first blow. Contaminate the earth in the boxes, so that he cannot return to his lair.

Morris   Drive him into the open, where we can face him outright?

Van Helsing   Exactly so, Mr Morris.

Seward   And then?

Van Helsing   Then, weakened by the sun's rays, we shall have him at our mercy – and, with weapons of goodness, and trust in God, we shall drive him at last from earth into hell where he belongs.

Holmwood   I wish I thought it would be as simple as it sounds.

Van Helsing   You're right to speak words of caution, Mr Holmwood. We must not underestimate his cunning and his intelligence. But I have reason to believe he has urgent business to hand. And his urgency may cause him to be careless – and in that may lie our advantage, and our victory.

Morris   The sun's going down.

Van Helsing	Then we must be about our business. Mrs Harker, you will stay here? I think it best you do.
Mina	Yes.
Van Helsing	And Mr Harker, you will remain with your wife. Safeguard the room from entry, as I've shown you.
Jonathan	I will.
Van Helsing	Go. Do it now.

Jonathan goes.

Van Helsing	Doctor Seward, Mr Holmwood, Mr Morris – make yourselves ready for this night's business. Our weapons are downstairs. I wish to speak with Mrs Harker privately a moment. I'll join you shortly.

Seward, Holmwood and Morris go. Van Helsing turns to Mina.

Van Helsing	He will come for you again tonight.
Mina	Again? You know?
Van Helsing	Yes. You wear a shawl about your neck. To hide the marks. And there are other signs that I have learned. It was last night?
Mina	Last night, yes.
Van Helsing	Does your husband know?
Mina	No. I hardly knew myself – I thought it was a bad dream – until I looked in the mirror.
Van Helsing	Are you strong enough to resist him?
Mina	I shall try to be.
Van Helsing	I know you shall. There is a quality within you that is rare. A strength, a courage of the soul. It is that which draws him to you. And it is that which will help to defeat him.

Mina

I pray to God it will.

Van Helsing

Just this one night, Mrs Harker. One night, and, with the dawn that follows, you shall be rid of him.

> ***Van Helsing*** *turns and goes.*
> ***Mina*** *remains onstage.*

. . . .

Scene 6

> ***Mina*** *speaks to the audience. As she does so, she draws back the curtain to reveal the French window.*

Mina

The sun set. Night came. I went to our room. Flowers of garlic were hung from the window frames. A crucifix stood, bravely, on the table. A smaller crucifix, on a chain, hung at my neck. But I knew they would all be to no avail. Already Jonathan lay, in a heavy sleep, across the bed. Already a mist was gathering outside. Already the room was filled with a sweet, heavy scent. And, as if from somewhere far off, or as if from somewhere deep inside, his voice spoke.

> ***Dracula*** *enters at the far side of the stage.*

Dracula

What are these trinkets against my power? This primitive magic has no authority over me.

> ***Mina*** *continues to speak to the audience.*

Mina

I took down the flowers of garlic from the window frame. I loosened the catch, pushed the glass wide. The night air touched my face, a soft sigh of content. But there was nothing beyond, nothing to be seen. Only thick mist, congealing to some outward form. I turned back to the room. I crossed to the bed and kissed Jonathan as he lay sleeping. I brushed the hair from his eyes. Then all collapsed, and was made new again, and I turned back, and he was there.

Dracula approaches Mina. He stops and speaks to her.

Dracula Remove that.

Mina (*To the audience*) He pointed to the crucifix at my neck. I took it off and dropped it to the floor.

Dracula Come here to me.

Mina (*To the audience*) I went across to him. I stood before him. His shadow was upon me, and my soul shivered.

Mina approaches Dracula.

Dracula You are afraid.

Mina Yes.

Dracula There is no need to be. No need to fear me.

Mina No need?

Dracula You think I bring you death, but I bring you life.

Mina I know what you bring. If it were death, I would welcome it. But it is neither life nor death. Something unholy, abominable –

Dracula (*Interrupting*) You know nothing of which you speak! Nothing! How could you know? My existence is... unimaginable to any of mortal flesh. The world you walk in, the world of light and sun that is your only reality, is to me a thing of mist and rags and shadows. It is frail as a spider's web compared to mine. For mine is a world eternal and unchanging, a world of bottomless depths and endless horizons. It is a world where silence has a voice, and sings the frozen void between the stars. This is my world. And it shall be yours.

Mina	Mine? What do you mean?
Dracula	For centuries I have walked my world alone. In fierce joy, but in weariness too. The weariness of solitude. For so long I have yearned for a companion to share with me this world, this eternity. So I shall walk alone no more. One shall walk beside me. You. You shall be my companion.
Mina	No –
Dracula	Listen! I could feed on you as I have fed on others. You would become undead, feed on others in your turn. Yet I sense in you a kinship, a likeness to myself. The same proud spirit, the same strong will. Is it not so? Do you not sense something of it yourself?

Mina says nothing.

Dracula	You do not deny it. You know. It is our destiny to walk together, to feed upon this world, devour it all. And so, I do not force you. I do not feed upon you. But ask you to come to me willingly. To become as I, equal and free. To feed upon me.

He holds out his hand to her.

Dracula	Come.

Mina takes a step towards him, then pulls back.

Mina	I will not! No!

Dracula snarls in rage.

Dracula	You shall not deny me! You shall be mine!
Mina	Perhaps. But never willingly.
Dracula	Then your husband is dead. Even as he lies there sleeping, I shall crush him, tear his throat, feed on him before your eyes –
Mina	No!

Dracula	Then come to me. Come to me and he lives. Though I hate him, I shall let him live, for you. Will you do this for him? Will you give him his life?

Mina pauses for a moment.

Mina	Yes. For love of him. For you I have nothing but hate.
Dracula	That will not be for long. Soon, he will be nothing to you. And I – we – shall be all.

He steps back from her.

Dracula	Come. Let us make our pact.

Mina turns and speaks to the audience. As she speaks, Dracula goes.

Mina	What that pact was, and how it was made, I have not told anyone, nor will ever tell. But there, in the dark of the room, it seemed my soul floated from my body, and crossed immense spaces, and I saw great forests and dark mountains, and a wide plain stretching between them. And all was sharp and clear and bright. And where the earth ended, the mountains rose, and there was yet more beyond the mountains, and I was running, and the horizons rolled beneath my feet, and there was no end to them.

Mina turns and goes.

. . . .

Scene 7

Jonathan enters and speaks to the audience.

Jonathan	They woke me in the early hours of the morning. Mina was still sleeping, and they called me out of the room, not to disturb her. There were only the two of them, and I could tell by their faces that something was terribly wrong.

> *Van Helsing and Seward enter and approach Jonathan. They are distressed, and in a state of fear and alarm.*

Van Helsing   Wrong, yes! All wrong! We should have known he could not be taken so easily.

Jonathan   What do you mean? Where are the others?

Seward   Dead.

Jonathan   No –

Van Helsing   I'm sorry, yes.

Jonathan   Tell me what happened.

Seward   We came to the Manor some time after sunset. All was dark and silent. Arthur and Quincey remained by the door, to keep watch. The Professor and I went inside, down to the cellar. We found the boxes. But there were only four.

Jonathan   Four? But –

Van Helsing   Two must have been removed to some other place for safety. It was then we realized that Dracula must have guessed our plans. Nonetheless, we set about our work. Removed the lids from the remaining boxes. Sprinkled holy water on the earth, placed crosses there, so that they were no longer refuge for the undead.

Seward   But then, just as we were finishing, we heard cries from above. We raced back up the stairs and outside, and there we saw… four… creatures… I still don't know what they were – wolf or human. It's impossible to say.

Van Helsing   They were creatures of hell, come at Dracula's bidding. And they had struck down those poor men, and were feeding upon them.

Jonathan   My God –

Seward	I heard them feeding, heard the sound of their jaws tearing and ripping. And then… then they looked up – and I saw their faces –
Van Helsing	They would have leapt on us too, torn out our throats. But the crucifix checked them. Armed with the holy weapon, we advanced, and they fell back snarling. Turned at last, and disappeared into the darkness of the wood.
Jonathan	And Arthur, and Quincey – ?
Seward	There was nothing we could do for them. Arthur was already dead. Quincey died as we knelt beside him.
Jonathan	Where are they now?
Van Helsing	We took their bodies into the house. I laid the crucifix upon them to protect them from further desecration. Tomorrow we must return, and give them a proper burial.
Jonathan	Yes… of course… but what's to be done now?
Van Helsing	I confess, I'm not certain… we have failed. He foresaw all, and led us into his trap. And he is still at large. We must… think again. For this is a foe indeed to be feared.

Jonathan, Seward and *Van Helsing go.*

. . . .

Scene 8

Mina enters and speaks to the audience.

Mina	So I knew at last that it must be me. When I learned from Professor Van Helsing and Doctor Seward what had happened, when I saw their weakened, exhausted faces, when I saw how the shock of it struck at Jonathan, brought back to him the horror of his own experiences – then I knew that I, and I alone, must destroy this monster. For what the monster was, I too was now in part. And the strength he had given me could be turned against him.

Mina pauses before continuing. As she
speaks Renfield enters, behind her.

Mina So I went back to where it had all begun. To the churchyard by the abbey, on the clifftop above the sea. And I thought of how Lucy and I had walked there, in the summer, how she'd told me of her engagement, how we'd talked and laughed together and planned our futures, and how full of life and love and hope we had both been. And I thought too of Mr Swales, and the storm, and the ship, and of the darkness that had come with the storm and the ship. And it seemed as I thought of those things, that as all had begun there, all the evil and horror, so there too it must end.

Cautiously, Renfield approaches Mina.

Renfield You've come to seek him?

Mina starts and turns to Renfield.

Mina Yes.

Renfield But you find only me.

Mina Where you are, he will not be far.

Renfield It's true – yes – he binds me to him – holds me fast – my soul in his fist – squeezing – 'You are free,' he said – but he knows I can never be free – not until –

Mina He is destroyed.

Renfield (*With sudden passion*) Yes! Destroyed! You will destroy him?

Mina If I can.

Renfield But you are – you are like him –

Mina No –

Renfield Of his kind –

Mina No –

Renfield   Yes! He has taken you to him. He is making you as he is. It works in you – the power – growing – the dark in your heart – the hunger –

Mina   Not yet! I fight it. I will destroy him, and destroy the darkness within me.

Renfield   Not alone. Too much of you belongs to him. At the end you would falter. But together, you and I –

Mina   (*Taken aback*) You?

Renfield   (*Determined*) Yes! I will be free of him at last. He burns in me, he scalds my soul! I wish to be – a man again.

Mina   You know where he is?

Renfield   There. In the abbey. The crypt. He lies there now. You go to him, walk with him in the dark. Keep him with you all night. I shall defile his earth, give him no sanctuary. Then, when the day comes, he will die. Go now. The sun is setting. He will rise soon, and you must be there to greet him.

Renfield goes. Mina speaks to the audience.

Mina   As the sky reddened I went to the abbey. As the last rays of light splashed upon its walls, I walked among its ruined stones, entered the broken doorway, descended to the dark beneath the earth. And there I found him.

> *Dracula* *enters and speaks to Mina.*

Dracula   I knew you would come.

> *Mina* *continues to tell her story to the audience.*

Mina   Together in the dark we stood, and I could feel part of me drawing towards him, longing to embrace the world of his making, the monstrous, the merciless, the unfettered. And that part I let go to him – but kept another secret, held precious and safe.

Dracula   (*To Mina*) Tonight I shall not feed. It is not yet necessary. We shall make our pact again. You shall draw blood from me once more, come closer to the eternal life.

Mina   (*Turning to speak to Dracula*) Yes. But not here. Outside, on the clifftop.

Dracula   The place you first saw me, when I fed on the other?

Mina   Yes, there.

Dracula   It's fitting. Where it began, it shall end. And a new life begin.

> *Mina* *turns back to speak to the audience.*

Mina   Such visions I saw that night. Wonders and terrors. I saw the ages of the world, saw how life in those ages flowered and withered, brief as a breath, an insect thing. And there, apart from it all, drawing life from the living, one creature unchanging. Myself. And I stood among the ruins of creation, and the earth was waste about me, and my soul cried out, and there was nothing to hear.

Dracula   (*To Mina*) It is almost finished now. You feel the power growing in you. Soon there will be nothing but that power. You will shed your mortality like a dry skin. And then you will know the rapture and the glory, the terrible joy, the insatiable hunger.

Mina	(*To the audience*) In the east, the sky was lightening. The morning wind blew in fresh from the sea. On the earth, the dew glimmered. In the sky, the stars dimmed.
Dracula	(*To Mina*) I must go now. Seek me out again tomorrow night. Then our pact shall be sealed, and together we shall hunt, and feed.

> ***Renfield** enters. He screams at Dracula in hatred.*

Renfield	No! You will never hunt or feed again!

> ***Dracula** wheels round to Renfield. **Mina** steps aside and watches the following scene with growing horror.*

Renfield	Never stalk the night earth, never prey upon the living. Never, never again! Not even flies and spiders, Master! See the light! See the sun! The master must go, he must seek his hiding place. Hide from the sun. But where? Where can he hide? Nowhere!
Dracula	What do you mean? What have you done?
Renfield	No sanctuary, no place of rest! All are closed to him now. Holy water, God's flesh. They drive him out, drive him to his death!
Dracula	You have betrayed me!
Renfield	Yes, Master. Poor Renfield! Wretched Renfield. Renfield who was nothing to you. You had done with me! Now I have done with you! She and I together. The one you cast aside, and the one you chose. We destroy you. The spider caught in his own web. Soon you'll be no more. All will be free, all that have been taken, free of you. I shall be free. I shall be a man again!

> *Swiftly and savagely, **Dracula** grabs Renfield by the throat. **Mina** cries out.*

Mina	No!

> *Mina runs to help Renfield but **Dracula** knocks her down. He squeezes Renfield by the throat. **Renfield** gasps, struggles, then falls silent and still. His body hangs heavy. **Dracula** lets him drop to the floor.*

Dracula   My last act in this world.

> *He turns and speaks to the audience.*

Dracula   Now let day come. Let the sun rise. Let the light of your world burn me to dust. It shall know me no more, and I leave it with my undying hate!

> ***Dracula** freezes. **Mina** rises, speaking to the audience as she does so.*

Mina   Then the sky burst into flame, and he gave a cry, a long howl of anguish and pain and rage and despair. And as it rose, the light seared through him, and he was gone, leaving nothing but dust that was taken by the wind and scattered across the face of the deep.

> *Blackout. In the blackout, there is a loud, terrifying cry, rising, echoing, then dying to silence.*

. . . .

Scene 9

> *The lights come up on an empty stage. **Van Helsing**, **Seward** and **Jonathan** enter on their lines, and stand one at either side, and one at the back of the stage. They speak to the audience.*

Van Helsing   So we had come through the flames and were purged of evil. Though it had cost us dear, the enemy had been defeated and good, as it always must, prevailed.

Seward
But the wounds of the battle had gone deep, and though some at last healed, we bore the scars always. All had lost something. None would ever be the same.

Jonathan
So we went back to what we could salvage of our lives. We settled, had children, lived comfortably, though not in great prosperity. And if ever we spoke of that desperate time, it was as of something long past and done with, for, in the end, we had peace of spirit and mind.

> ***Mina*** *enters and stands centre stage. She speaks to the audience.*

Mina
But still even now I dream. And in my dream I'm standing beneath a great expanse of sky, lit by numberless stars, and ahead of me is a wide grassland, stretching out into the distance where the black shadows of mountains rise. And all is clear and sharp and bright, and there's such silence, such longing, and the moon is full and we are wolves and we are running, and the horizons roll endlessly beneath our feet.

Activities

About the Author

Bram Stoker was born in November 1847 in Dublin. As a child, he was ill and spent long hours in bed. During this time, his mother Charlotte told him Irish fairy stories and true accounts of the horrors of the cholera epidemic she had witnessed during her own childhood. No one really knows what was wrong with Bram, but he made a complete recovery and grew to be a fit and energetic young man.

In 1864, Stoker went to Trinity college, Dublin where he became a popular student and a good athlete. He also developed a passion for the theatre. In 1867, he saw the famous actor Henry Irving performing at the Theatre Royal, Dublin. This experience had a huge and lasting effect on Bram Stoker.

After gaining his degree, he became a civil servant. But in 1871 he saw Irving again at the Vaudeville Theatre. He was so impressed with Irving's performance that he decided to become a theatre critic and offered his services free of charge to the *Dublin Mail.*

About this time he began to take an interest in vampires. He read vampire stories by other authors and started to think about writing his own vampire tale. In 1875 he published his first 'horror' story – *The Chain of Destiny.*

In 1876, Henry Irving returned to Dublin to play Hamlet. Stoker wrote glowing reviews of Irving's performance which led to a meeting between the two. Irving asked Stoker to become his business manager in London. Before leaving Dublin, Stoker resigned from the civil service and married Florence Balcombe, a neighbour who had also been courted by the writer Oscar Wilde.

Stoker worked long hours for Irving, but he still made time to continue his research on vampires and other 'gothic' themes. He continued to write horror stories for adults and children. In 1890 he started work on **Dracula**. During the next few years he spent summer holidays at Whitby in North Yorkshire and at Cruden Bay in Scotland. Both places were to influence descriptions and events in the novel he was writing. **Dracula** was published in 1897.

In 1905, Henry Irving collapsed and died. This had a dramatic effect on Stoker who suffered a stoke. His employer's death signalled the end of his contract and so Stoker had to write more fiction to earn a living. He finished his final novel, *The Lair of the White Worm,* in 1911. He died a year later from 'exhaustion' aged 64.

Reactions to the Novel

When **Dracula** was published in 1897, Charlotte Stoker wrote this to her son:

> 'No book since Mrs Shelley's *Frankenstein* or indeed any other at all has come near yours in originality or terror – Poe is nowhere... In its terrible excitement it should make a widespread reputation and much money for you.'

She wasn't the only person to admire the work. Stoker knew what his audience wanted and delivered it. The reviews were very positive:

> 'It is horrid and creepy to the last degree.'

> 'Its fascination is so great that it is impossible to lay it aside.'

> '...a triumph for the writer... the interest of the danger, of the complications, of the pursuit of the villain, of human skill and courage pitted against inhuman wrong and superhuman strength, rises always to the top.'

It was also a hit with the young Winston Churchill and the elderly William Gladstone, the former Liberal Prime Minister, who told the author it was 'very successful in maintaining the reader's interest in the story'.

Discuss

Originally, Bram Stoker's novel had another title. What alternative title do you suggest?

Design

Plan an advertisement for the original novel. Your target audience is readers of the late 1890s. How can you persuade people to buy and read **Dracula**? Think about the design – what text and images will you use? You could use some of the comments from reviewers printed above. How can you combine your choice of words and pictures to produce a powerful advert?

Stoker's Sources for the Novel

Read

Bram Stoker had been fascinated by vampires for some years before he started to write **Dracula**. By the end of the Nineteenth century, there was a great interest in and demand for literature dealing with crime, horror and the supernatural: the 1880s and 90s saw the publication of *The Strange Tale of Dr Jekyll and Mr Hyde*, *The Picture of Dorian Gray*, *The Adventures of Sherlock Holmes*, and *The War of the Worlds*. Other novels about vampires had been published, and we know that Bram Stoker had read some of them. But he was also inspired by

- stories from vampire folklore
- his historical research of the life of Vlad Dracula or Vlad Tepes (Vlad the Impaler).

He set his story in real places: London, Whitby, and Transylvania (the area found now in Northern Romania).

Vampire Folklore

Read

Stoker spent many hours researching the vampire legends from Eastern Europe. The vampire described in folklore is a rough, evil creature who sleeps during the day and rises from the grave at night to torment living relatives and to search for victims – both animals and humans. It can appear in many forms – as a human, a dog, a wolf, a bat, or a bird – attacking and smothering its prey before feasting on its blood.

The peasants of Eastern Europe had a number of methods for protecting themselves from vampires.

- They rubbed garlic on their windows and doors, on their animals and themselves, believing that it had special powers to keep away evil.
- They sprinkled rose thorns and poppy seeds between the churchyard and the village, so that any vampire leaving its grave would stop to pick them up and count them. This would keep the vampire busy until dawn when it would have to return to the churchyard.
- They protected themselves and their homes with crucifixes and other Christian symbols.
- They believed that vampires were afraid of light.
- There were three ways to kill a vampire: drive a stake through its heart; burn it; or behead it!

Prince Vlad Dracula

Read

Bram Stoker was also very interested in the life of a fifteenth-century prince called Vlad Dracula. Vlad Dracula (meaning 'son of the dragon') was born in Transylvania but ruled over a province called Wallachia (now Southern Romania). In some historical reports he is considered to be a hero because of his success in defeating the Turkish invaders, but he also was known for his extreme cruelty. Legend had it, his favourite way of killing his enemies was to spear their bodies on sharp stakes. He liked to do this on a grand scale by building 'forests' of impaled victims as a warning to others who might try to overthrow him. This earned him the name of 'Vlad Tepes' which translated means 'Vlad the Impaler'. There is no suggestion that this Dracula was a vampire, but Bram Stoker certainly borrowed his name and gave it to his Transylvanian count.

Two portraits of Prince Vlad Dracula. The one on the left was made in 1485, nearly ten years after the Prince's death. The one on the right dates from 1500 and shows how he got his gruesome nickname!

Transylvania

Read

Although Bram Stoker never visited Transylvania, he read widely about its folklore, history and geography. The town of Bistritz (Bistrita), the Carpathian Mountains, and the Borgo Pass are all real places and can be found on modern maps of Romania as well as old maps of Transylvania. Castle Dracula also exists and, although it is in ruins, it is thought by local people to be the castle of Vlad the Impaler. However, it is nowhere near the site of the fictional Castle Dracula in the novel.

It also seems possible that Stoker didn't base his fictional Castle Dracula on the real one, but on a painting of another Transylvanian fortress, Castle Bran, built in the Thirteenth century high above the surrounding countryside. Although Castle Bran is also a long way from the fictional Castle Dracula, its description is very similar to Stoker's castle, and it has become part of the Dracula tourist route offered by the Romanian Tourist Ministry. It has also been used as a location for the making of Dracula films.

Castle Bran in Romania.

Research

Plan a web-site for one of the three topics you have just read about:

- Vampire folklore
- Vlad the Impaler
- Transylvania.

You can use the information given as a starting point – but the real challenge is to find new and varied material on your chosen topic. Be prepared to find out more facts – but also look for photographs, documents, maps, music, etc.

Dracula in the Play

Brainstorm

Before you read the playscript, what did you know about Dracula? In a group, brainstorm all the things you knew about Dracula – his looks, his clothes, his actions.

Read and Discuss

Re-read the Prologue. This is your first encounter with Dracula in the playscript.
1 What impression do you get of Dracula from these opening words?
2 How does this compare with your opinion of Dracula before you read the playscript?

Jonathan Harker's View

Jonathan Harker is the first person in the playscript to meet Dracula.

Read, List, Hot Seat

1 Re-read Act 1, Scene 1 and imagine that you can interview Jonathan Harker to get his first impressions about Count Dracula.
2 Make a list of questions you would like to ask Jonathan about the Count and his home.
3 Choose someone from the class to take the role of Jonathan Harker. Put him in the hot seat and ask him the questions you have prepared.
4 Then re-read Act 1, Scene 3 and put Jonathan back in the hot seat. Has his view of Dracula changed? How does he feel about him now?

You could use this hot-seating activity as a starting point for the letter activity on page 122.

Mina Harker's View

Mina first sees Dracula as the shadowy figure who threatens Lucy during her illness. She then hears about him from Jonathan who tells her all about his terrible ordeal at the castle in Transylvania. On returning to England at the beginning of Act 3, she learns that Lucy is dead and begins to suspect that there is some connection between Jonathan's experiences at Castle Dracula and Lucy's tragic end.

Write

Write an extract from Mina's diary in which she records what she knows of Count Dracula and the part he has played in the lives of her husband and her best friend. What are her feelings towards him at this point in the playscript?

Read, List, Hot Seat

1 By Act 3, Scene 5 we know that Mina has met Dracula. As a class, or in groups, re-read scenes 5-9.
2 Make a list of the questions you would like to ask Mina about Dracula and the events described in the final scenes of the playscript.
3 Choose someone from the class to be Mina. Put her in the hot seat and ask her the questions on your list. Can she answer them all? Do you think she always tells the truth?

Write and Discuss

1 Now imagine you are Mina and write another entry for your diary based on the events which take place at the end of the playscript. Before writing, read carefully Mina's last speech on page 105. Using the information from the hot-seating and your own impressions, write down Mina's true feelings about Dracula. Remember, this is a private diary, so make it as detailed and honest as you can.
2 Read a selection of the diaries aloud and discuss as a class what Mina really thinks of Dracula. Does she hate him and believe that he is a monster, or does part of her feel something else for him – attraction, pity, sympathy?

Renfield's View

Write and Discuss

Work in pairs or groups.
1 Write a list of questions that you would like to ask Renfield about Dracula.
2 What kind of answers do you think he would give?
3 Brainstorm some ideas about how you think Dracula and Renfield first met.
4 Then, write a flashback scene for the playscript which shows their first meeting. You can add new characters if you wish. You might choose to explain how Renfield ended up in Doctor Seward's asylum.

The Hero?

Debate

Who is the hero of the play? Mina? Renfield? Van Helsing? Dracula himself?
1 Start by thinking about the following questions.
   ● What makes a hero?
   ● Can a character who does evil things be a hero?
2 Make a list of all the possible candidates for the role of hero within the playscript. Then invite members of the class to speak in support of each of the people on the list.

3 Then vote on your choice for hero of the playscript. Is there an
   outright winner or is it a close run thing?

Interview with the Adapter

Read

David Calcutt's adaptation is different from Bram Stoker's original novel in several ways. Read this interview with the adapter, in which he explains how he tackled the adaptation.

When you started writing this adaptation, what was the first thing you had to think about?

One of the first challenges I faced when I started out was how to make this adaptation of **Dracula** different from every version that had come before. It's not that I believe in changing things, or making things different simply for the sake of it. But there have been so many versions of Bram Stoker's novel, for the stage, the radio and – most widely and popularly – for the screen, that the Count himself has become almost a cliché. Also, quite apart from **Dracula**, recently there has been a revival of interest in vampire stories generally – mainly in film and television – and each of these versions has explored the legend in its own way. When I started out, I really did wonder whether there was anything new to say about the subject.

So where did you begin?

Well, the job of an adapter isn't simply to re-tell the original story in play form. The adapter must engage with the story, find something in it that connects with his or her own interests – even obsessions. However faithfully you follow the original, it's inevitable that your version will be coloured by your own particular vision of that story and its themes. The Dracula of Bram Stoker's novel isn't the suave charmer who appears in later films. He's a beast, a monster without a soul. I felt the Dracula who appears in the novel was two-dimensional – he's not a fully-developed character. I wanted to know why Dracula was doing what he was doing. I wanted to tell some of the story from his viewpoint. Bram Stoker's novel is very much a product of its time: for the Victorians, Dracula was a thing of pure evil, to be destroyed at all cost. But we've come to see what we call 'evil' in a different light. We condemn it, but we also try to understand what causes it – what makes a person evil.

It sounds as though your Dracula's quite different from Bram Stoker's.

I think he is. The Dracula in the play is much less clear-cut, much more ambiguous, than the Dracula in the novel. His actions are horrific, but at the same time we can feel sorry for him. And he also holds out to Mina the promise of eternal life, complete freedom. At the end of the play, she's had a glimpse of something she can never forget. She's started to understand Dracula.

The novel of *Dracula* is huge – almost four hundred pages long. Was that a problem for you when you wrote the adaptation?
Definitely. The novel is packed and crowded with incident, character and detail, far too much and far too complex to include in a play. A play by its nature needs to be clear, simple and precise – otherwise it loses its focus, its drama. So, the next problem was, what to cut, what to leave out, and how to shape the story around a few intense dramatic moments? For a long time I didn't know and made several false starts. Whenever that happens, I decide that the only way out of the corner I've got myself into, is to take drastic action.

So what did you do?
I decided to pull the whole novel inside-out, so to speak, and start the play halfway through the original story, with Mina and Lucy in England. This had the desired effect. It helped make the play in part my own creation, and I was able to start writing seriously.

But this isn't how the play begins now, is it?
That's right. In the end I actually went back more or less to the original structure of the novel – starting with Jonathan's journey to Castle Dracula – but that initial kick-start had the effect of placing the two women, and especially Mina, at the centre of the action. And this made me realize that, in my version at least, the central dramatic conflict would be between Mina and Dracula, and that it would be Mina, not the men, who would finally bring about Dracula's defeat and destruction. I was very excited by this idea, and felt that, at last, I'd found a fresh way of looking at the story, a way to revitalize it, and re-make it as if new. Then I discovered that one of the first film versions of the novel – a silent film of the 1920s called *Nosferatu* – had done just this very thing! So, perhaps there are no new ways of looking at things after all. Only old ways.

Adapting Dracula

David Calcutt made several important changes when he adapted
Dracula for the stage:
- the locations used
- the character of Dracula himself
- the death of Renfield and the end of the play.

You are now going to look more closely at these changes.

Locations

Much of the action of the novel takes place in London in
recognizable places in and around the city. However, the adapter,
David Calcutt decided to set most of his play in only two of the
geographical locations used in the novel – Transylvania and Whitby.

Discuss

Why do you think he chose to do this?

The Dracula of the Novel

Read and Discuss

At first, Bram Stoker's Dracula appears to be an elderly aristocrat,
but as the novel progresses, he becomes increasingly beast-like and
monstrous. This extract, from Doctor Seward's diary, takes place
towards the end of the novel when the hunt for Dracula is on.

> Suddenly with a single bound he leaped into the room, winning a way
> past us before any of us could raise a hand to stay him. There was
> something panther-like in the movement – something so unhuman,
> that it seemed to sober us all from the shock of his coming... As the
> Count saw us, a horrible sort of snarl passed over his face, showing
> the eye-teeth long and pointed; but the evil smile as quickly passed
> into a cold stare of lion-like disdain. His expression again changed, as,
> with a single impulse, we all advanced upon him... [Now it was] so
> hellish that for a moment I feared for Harker... Instinctively I moved
> forward with a protective impulse, holding the crucifix and wafer in
> my left hand... I saw the monster cower back... It would be
> impossible to describe the expression of hate and baffled malignity –
> of anger and hellish rage – which came over the Count's face. His
> waxen hue became greenish-yellow by the contrast of his burning
> eyes, and the red scar on the forehead showed on the pallid skin like a
> palpitating wound. The next instant, with a sinuous dive he swept
> under Harker's arm, ...and, grasping a handful of money from the

floor, dashed across the room, threw himself at the window... We ran over and saw him spring unhurt from the ground.

1 Pick out all the words and phrases from the extract that suggest that Dracula is now seen as a beast or monster. (You may need to look some of the words up in a dictionary to be sure of their meaning.)
2 Go back to the playscript. What is the final view of Dracula there?
3 How does this compare with your first impressions of Dracula when you read the Prologue? (See activity on page 112.) Has your view changed and if so, in what way?
4 What is your overall view of the Dracula in the playscript? Do you pity him or hate him?

Renfield's Death

In the play, the events which lead to Renfield's death are rather different to those in the novel.

Read and Discuss

1 In a group, re-read Act 3, Scenes 4 and 8 of the playscript.
2 Then discuss this question: Why does Renfield want to kill Dracula?

Read

In the novel, Doctor Seward eventually realizes, through his conversations with Renfield, that there is a link between Dracula and Renfield. As Doctor Seward, Professor Van Helsing, Arthur Holmwood, Quincey Morris, and Jonathan get closer to destroying Dracula, Renfield's behaviour becomes increasingly erratic and so Doctor Seward decides to put a guard outside his room.

This is how Doctor Seward describes the events that follow in his diary:

> The attendant came bursting into my room and told me that Renfield had somehow met with some accident. He had heard him yell; and when he went to him found him lying on his face on the floor, all covered with blood. I must go at once...

Jonathan Harker then takes up the story in his journal:

> First, Doctor Seward told us that when he and Dr Van Helsing had gone down to the room below they had found Renfield lying on the floor, all in a heap. His face was all bruised and crushed in, and the bones of the neck were broken. Doctor Seward asked the attendant who was on duty in the passage if he had heard anything. He said that he had been sitting down – he confessed to half dozing – when he

heard loud voices in the room, and then Renfield had called out loudly several times, 'God! God! God!' After that there was a sound of falling, and when he had entered the room he found him lying on the floor, face down, just as the doctors had seen him. Van Helsing asked if he had heard 'voices' or a 'voice', and he said he could not say; that at first it had seemed to him as if there were two, but as there was no one in the room it could have only been one.

Renfield does not die immediately and lives long enough to tell Doctor Seward what Dracula is doing to Mina. (This is also recorded in Doctor Seward's diary.)

'When Mrs Harker came to see me this afternoon she wasn't the same; it was like tea after the teapot had been watered! ...I don't care for pale people; I like them with lots of blood in them, and hers had all seemed to have run out. I didn't think of it at the time, but when she went away I began to think, and it made me mad to know that he had been taking the life out of her... So when he came tonight I was ready for him...'

Discuss

What do you think that Renfield planned to do when Dracula arrived?

Write

Write a playscript scene of the novel's version of Renfield's death. Use the information from Doctor Seward and Jonathan's diaries and your discussion from the activity above.

Discuss

1 Compare Renfield's death in the novel with his death in the playscript. What are the differences between the two? You could look at:
   - what happens before his death
   - where his death takes place
   - who else witnesses his death
   - how he dies.
2 Which version of Renfield's death do you prefer and why?
3 Do you think the character of Renfield in the novel is different to the character of Renfield in the playscript?

Dracula's Escape

In the playscript, Dracula is eventually defeated in the grounds of the abbey on the clifftop in Whitby. In the novel, the men chase Dracula all over London looking for his hiding places. He outwits them and escapes on a boat to Transylvania. Doctor Seward, Professor Van Helsing, Arthur Holmwood, Quincey Morris, Jonathan, and Mina follow his trail, and confront him at the Castle. They must drive a stake through his heart before the sun sets. If they do not kill him, Mina will be a vampire forever.

Group Work

1 In a group, plan an ending to the story which follows Bram Stoker's original – with a final conflict at Castle Dracula. (The information in Act 1 of the playscript will give you some background information to Jonathan's travels in Transylvania and his stay at Castle Dracula. You may also want to add your own research about the country of Transylvania to help you write this piece.)

2 Write out your plot in note form. You may want to experiment with several versions before you decide which one you will follow.

3 Decide how you will present your alternative ending to the rest of the class. It could be as a dramatized reading or a wall display.

Remember, if you're doing a dramatized reading, you will have to produce a script or a written narrative of the story. You'll need to decide whose viewpoint you will use to tell the story – Mina, Van Helsing, or one of the other men? You can use more than one viewpoint if you like, in the way that Bram Stoker does.

You will also have to decide how you are going to split the writing between the members of your group. Will you have each member of the group writing a different section, or will you elect someone to do all the writing while the rest of the group suggests words and phrases?

The Structure of the Novel

Read

In Bram Stoker's **Dracula**, the storyline is not told from a single viewpoint. Like in *The Woman in White* by Wilkie Collins – a popular mystery story written in 1861 – it has a number of narrators. Stoker allows his narrators to use a wide range of techniques by which to record their stories including:

- journals
- diaries (Doctor Seward's diary is kept in a phonograph, a machine capable of recording and reproducing sound)
- letters between friends
- business letters
- telegrams
- cuttings from newspaper reports
- the ship's log of the *Demeter*
- medical reports
- memos and notes.

It is also interesting that Stoker's characters use the most modern forms of communication available to them at the end of the Nineteenth century – such as the typewriter, the stenograph (a machine with a keyboard for writing in shorthand), the phonograph, photographs and telegrams.

In the playscript, the story unfolds in two ways:
- through a number of narrators who speak to the audience describing events from the past
- by the dramatization of actual events in real time.

As it is impossible to include every detail from the novel in the playscript, there are times when we are left to imagine some of the details of the story. Here is your opportunity to 'fill in' some of these details through letters, reports, and other records – as Bram Stoker did in his novel.

Letters between Count Dracula and Mr Hawkins

Write

Playscript reference: Act 1, Scene 1.
Remember these are business letters between a foreign aristocrat and an English solicitor. Plan your letters carefully and keep the tone formal. You might like to create an appropriate letterhead for the firm of solicitors and a family crest for Count Dracula's writing paper.

1 Write the Count's letter stating his wish to move to England and instructing the solicitor, Mr Hawkins, to find him a suitable property.
2 Write Mr Hawkins's letter to Count Dracula describing a suitable property.
3 Then write Dracula's reply asking Mr Hawkins to travel with all the documents to Transylvania.
4 Finally, write Mr Hawkins's letter to Count Dracula introducing Jonathan and explaining that he will handle the business from now on.

Letters between Jonathan and Mina

Write

Playscript references: Act 1, Scenes 1-4 and Act 2, Scenes 1 and 3.
These are informal, personal letters between two people who are soon to be married.

1 Write a series of letters from Jonathan to Mina during his stay at Castle Dracula to explain his delay and then his fear that he is being kept a prisoner. (Dracula intercepts these letters and so Mina never receives them.)
2 Write the letters that Mina sends to Jonathan (via Mr Hawkins) describing her stay in Whitby with Lucy.

Doctor Seward's Medical Reports on Renfield

Write

Playscript references: Act 2, Scene 2 and Act 3, Scenes 2 and 5.
You could write these reports or record them onto tape. The reports should cover:
- Doctor Seward's own observations of Renfield
- individual statements made by Renfield's attendants, Bennett and Withers, on his behaviour
- Doctor Seward's report on Renfield's escape.

Newspaper Reports

Write

Imagine you are the journalist writing the newspaper stories for the events described below. Don't forget to:
- invent dramatic headlines
- follow the 'golden rule' of journalism and answer the five Ws (who, what, when, where and why)

- use quotations from eye-witnesses, experts and other interested parties.

Write reports on:
1 the storm and the arrival of the *Demeter* in Whitby harbour (Act 2, Scene 1)
2 the disappearance of local children from the area around the old abbey and graveyard (Act 2, Scene 6)
3 the escape of a dangerous inmate from the town's asylum (Act 3, Scenes 4 and 5).

Dracula: The Story Continues…

Dracula and the Movies

Most people's impression of **Dracula** has been gained from films and TV adaptations. Here are just some of the visual interpretations of **Dracula** which have appeared since the publication of the novel in 1897.

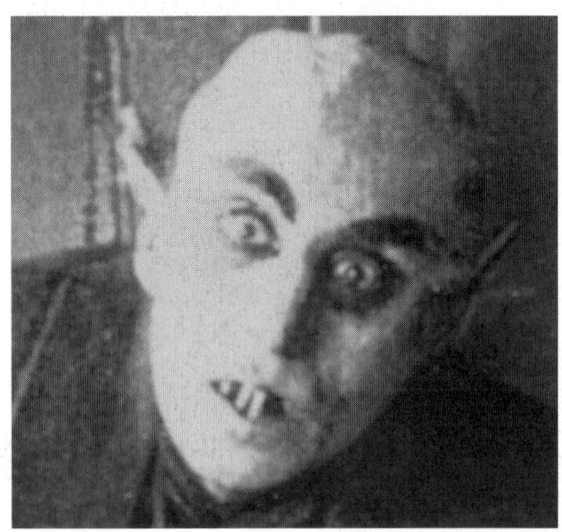

◀ In 1922, a German black and white film, directed by W.F. Murnau and called *Nosferatu, The Vampire* starred Max Schreck as the vampire, Count Orlock. The script was based on Bram Stoker's novel, with changes to the setting of the story and the names of the characters.

▼ The first 'talking' version of *Dracula* was released in 1931. It starred Bela Lugosi as Count Dracula and was directed by Tod Browning.

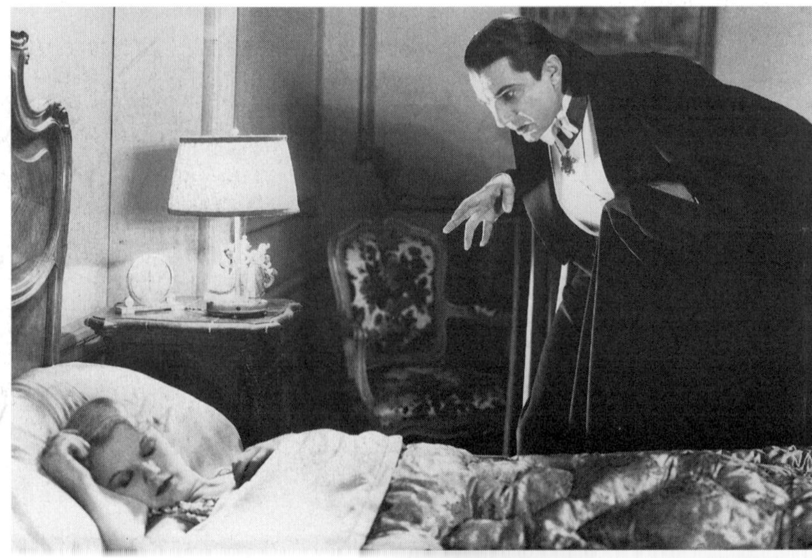

▼ Francis Ford Coppola's film *Bram Stoker's Dracula* was released in 1992 and stared Gary Oldman and Winona Ryder.

▲ In 1958, Christopher Lee made the first of many appearances as Dracula in Terence Fisher's *Horror of Dracula*. He is probably the actor most people associate with the role of Dracula. His face appears on the cover of this book.

► It hasn't all been serious stuff. In 1979, George Hamilton played the Count in a very successful spoof on the Dracula story.

And people still turn up in huge numbers dressed in outrageous clothes for the vampire rock musical, *The Rocky Horror Show*.

Dracula Spin-offs

Vampires are extremely popular in youth culture. They appear in books, TV adaptations, comics, films, cartoons, advertisements – the list is endless. There are scary vampires, cute vampires, vampires to make you laugh, vampires to make you scream and vampires to fall in love with.

Brainstorm

1　In groups, brainstorm as many titles and/or names as you can from the list below. They must all have vampire connections and be aimed at young people under the age of 16. Don't forget material aimed at much younger children – you may need to ask people with younger brothers and sisters for some help here. Think about:
   - books
   - films/videos
   - TV programmes
   - fictional characters.
2　Which vampire books, films, and TV series are the most popular at the moment?
3　Who are the favourite authors/characters?

Count Duckula, from the children's TV series.

Research

You may find it helpful to do this work in your local children's library.

1 Choose a book on a vampire theme suitable for a primary school child.
2 Read it and make notes on the following questions:
   - What kind of book is this? (Fiction or non-fiction? Serious or humorous?)
   - Who is it aimed at?
   - What is its purpose?
   - Name the main character(s).
   - How would you describe them?
   - Is it a good read for its target age group?
   - Did you enjoy it? Explain why you did/did not.

Watch and Discuss

Buffy, the Vampire Slayer first appeared as a film in 1992. This was the springboard for a hugely popular TV series (also available on video), aimed at young people aged 12 and over.

Watch an episode of *Buffy, the Vampire Slayer* and answer the following questions.
- Who is Buffy and what is her mission?
- What tools does she use in her fight against vampires?
- What else did you learn about vampires from this episode?
- What other creatures is she required to 'slay'?
- Why do you think this series is so popular?

Write

Write a vampire story set in your town. This can be serious horror, a spoof or something between the two. Use 'real' places to make the location convincing. Unusual natural landscapes and interesting buildings can create a great atmosphere. But remember, ordinary places work well too. When the horror lurks within a familiar environment like a library or a school it can be more scary than a spooky old castle.

The Dracula Experience

There is no doubt that Bram Stoker visited Whitby. He spent several holidays there and also used the library to research material for **Dracula**. Visitors to this small fishing town can now follow the 'Dracula Trail'. This takes them past the house where Lucy and Mina stayed, across the bridge to Tate Hill harbour where they can look down on the sands where the *Demeter* came ashore, up the 199 steps to the churchyard and so to the dramatic clifftop ruins of Whitby Abbey. The town is popular with admirers of Count Dracula and his story, and it is not unusual to see white-faced figures dressed in long, black cloaks wandering around the churchyard.

Dracula enthusiasts can also enjoy the 'Bram Stoker Dracula Experience'. During this 'eerie spine chilling show' with 'lifelike models', the visitor can see scenes from the novel – including an 'animated ship' and 'opening coffins'.

Discuss and Design

Work in groups. You have won the contract to design a Dracula theme park close to Whitby. Use the events, geographical locations and characters from the playscript as inspiration for your project.

1 Study a map to choose a convenient location. This should not be far from good road and rail links.
2 Draw a plan of the park to show
   - the attractions – rides, other play areas, performance spaces, etc.
   - wet-weather facilities
   - refreshment zones – to include restaurants, cafes, kiosks and picnic areas
   - parking
   - anything else you consider to be important.
3 Provide notes, plans and drawings of individual attractions and/or rides.
4 Design and produce a publicity leaflet to attract families and **Dracula** enthusiasts to your park.

NOTE: Bram Stoker's original title for **Dracula** was *The Un-Dead.*